Charles Dickens

INSPIRATIONS SERIES

Series Editor: Rosemary Goring

An easy-to-read series of books
that introduce people of achievement whose
lives are inspirational.

Other titles in the series:

Muhammad Ali
Robert Burns
Bob Dylan
John Lennon
Nelson Mandela
J. K. Rowling
The Williams Sisters

Further titles to follow in 2012

Charles Dickens

Hard Times and Great Expectations

Alan Taylor

ARGYLL ✠ PUBLISHING

© Alan Taylor 2011

Argyll Publishing
Glendaruel
Argyll PA22 3AE
Scotland
www.argyllpublishing.co.uk

**British Library
Cataloguing-in-
Publication Data.**

**A catalogue record for
this book is available
from the British Library.**

ISBN 978 1 906134 67 9

ALBA | CHRUTHACHAIL

Printing:
Martins the Printers,
Berwick upon Tweed

CONTENTS

INTRODUCTION

IN 1841, when he was 29 years of age and at the height of his powers and fame, Charles Dickens visited Edinburgh. To coin a word soon to be in common usage, he was a celebrity. Already he had written *The Pickwick Papers*, *Nicholas Nickleby*, *Oliver Twist* and *The Old Curiosity Shop*, all of which were bestsellers and would ensure their author's place in the literary hall of fame.

Eagerly anticipating his journey north from London, where he was constantly on call and on show, Dickens declared, 'I am on the highest crag of expectation.' Edinburgh was not entirely foreign terrain for him. His wife Catherine was from Edinburgh and he had visited the Scottish capital seven years earlier as a young reporter.

On that occasion he had travelled by boat, an experience he had no desire to repeat. This time he and

Catherine let the train, a relatively novel form of transport, take part of the strain. Edinburgh was no less keen to see Dickens than he it. Everyone who was anyone wanted to meet him and his schedule was jam-packed with engagements. At one dinner 270 people dined while 200 others, mostly women, watched them. Simply to be able to say you'd seen Dickens put a fork in his mouth was, it seems, enough to make some swoon. As the great writer entered the room the band played 'Charlie Is My Darling' and cheers rang out.

Writing to his future biographer, John Forster, Dickens could hardly contain his astonishment at the reaction to his presence in the sooty Scottish capital. 'The hotel is perfectly besieged,' he wrote, 'and I have been forced to take refuge in a sequestered apartment at the end of a long passage, wherein I write this letter.' The image evoked is that of a rock star stalked by his adoring, hysterical fans. In the days that followed he was given the freedom of the city, an honour usually bestowed on men at least twice as old, and taken wherever he wanted to go, including Loch Katrine and the island of the 'Lady of the Lake' in the Trossachs, the setting for one of Sir Walter Scott's most popular poems.

But despite all the sightseeing and hobnobbing, eating and drinking, Dickens continued to work. For him writing was like breathing, and as natural. In an era when there were no mechanical aids – no ballpoint pens, no typewriters, no word processors, no laptops, no broadband or Google – writing was a profession that required remarkable powers of endurance and application, both of which Dickens had in abundance. He could write when on the move and in the most trying of circumstances, when, say, the light was fading or he was surrounded by noisy crowds. As a reporter he had been required to write come what may. At that stage, not writing was never an option. If he wanted to be paid, if he wanted to maintain the lifestyle to which he had become accustomed, he had to meet deadlines and write however many words were demanded of him.

It was, as he might have said himself, the best of times and the worst of times. The pressure was immense, the stress nerve-jangling, but with his adrenalin high and his ambition boundless, Dickens could always be relied upon to rise to the occasion.

Nor did he change when he swapped journalism for fiction. While in Edinburgh he was working on his next project, *Barnaby Rudge*, his fifth novel, which at least in part was inspired by Scott's *The Heart of Midlothian*. As with so much of what Dickens wrote, however, it was rooted firmly in his childhood.

Every writer, consciously or not, directly or indirectly, wholly or partially, plunders his past and reinvents it to his own convenience. The novelist L.P. Hartley said, 'The past is a foreign country; they do things differently there.' Indeed they do. But a writer's past is very familiar territory. It is a place he knows well and is inhabited by people whose language he speaks and whose way of life he understands because he is one of them. To Dickens the past, *his* past, was like a fire in a volcano, inextinguishable, unforgettable, liable to erupt and consume him when he least expected. As we shall see in the pages that follow it made him who he was, most of which was ultimately to his benefit, but a lot of which scarred and damaged and haunted him.

The specific part of his past with which Dickens was concerned in *Barnaby Rudge* was Newgate Prison in London. In Victorian Britain prisons figured hugely and Dickens was more aware of them than most, not least because his father spent time in one. As a schoolboy he would often pass Newgate, with its massive walls and gates, and would be overcome with a sense of foreboding and despair. Inside, as Dickens knew only too well, were men who had committed crimes, some terrible, some – by modern standards – minor, who were awaiting execution by hanging.

For him, therefore, Newgate held a 'horrible fascination' and gripped his imagination, appearing not just in *Barnaby Rudge* but also in *Oliver Twist* and *Great Expectations*, in which its hero Pip, one of Dickens's several alter egos, is shown inside 'the grim stone buildings', to view the yard where the gallows are kept and 'the Debtors' Door out of which culprits come to be hanged'.

This, though, is to get ahead of ourselves. Thinking of Dickens at this point in his life it is easy to see him as someone who has it all, that all he need do now is nurture his success and protect his reputation and all will be well. Like many who achieve fame and fortune at a young age Dickens could not help but revel in it. He could, too, have been excused for feeling complacent and smug, even arrogant.

Dickens was not like that. Rather he was a writer who understood that he was only as good as his next book, that whatever he achieved, whether the riches accrued from bestsellerdom or the plaudits of critics, could disappear like sun when shrouded in cloud. For the greatest literary genius of the nineteenth century there could be no standing still, no resting on laurels, no soaking up of applause. For in order to live he had to write. It was as simple and as complex as that.

Charles Dickens

CHAPTER ONE
Growing Up

'If you really want to hear about it, the first
thing you'll probably want to know is where I
was born and what my lousy childhood was
like, and how my parents were occupied and all
before they had me, all that David Copperfield
kind of crap, but I don't feel like going into it, if
you want to know the truth.'

THESE words are not, of course, those of Charles
Dickens. Or of one of his characters. They come
from the mouth of Holden Caulfield and were put there
by J.D. Salinger, author of *The Catcher in the Rye*.
Holden is a rebel and wants nothing to do with anything
he regards as phony or which smacks of authority.

Where David Copperfield fits into this is not at all
clear. What is clear, however, is that Holden Caulfield
and David Copperfield have more in common than might

first be assumed, both being boys cast adrift and making their way in a world in which lurk dangers unspecified, and adults must be viewed with suspicion if not fear.

It was an attitude of mind that the young Dickens himself shared. The world in which he grew up, a world that seemed to be constantly in flux, in which more children died before they reached their teens than survived beyond them, was one that did not inspire confidence in the future. Nor did his family's circumstances offer much by way of consolation or security for his was a childhood over which hung the ready threat of disappointment and deprivation.

Here then, ignoring Holden Caulfield's self-inflicted advice, are a few hard facts about Dickens's childhood which, if truth be told, was sometimes pretty lousy. He was born on 7th February, 1812, the same year that marked the beginning of the American War of Independence and Napoleon's disastrous assault on Russia, and christened Charles John Huffam Dickens.

The town of Portsmouth, on England's south coast, was his birthplace. His father was John Dickens who worked in the Naval Pay Office; his mother was called Elizabeth and she had married her husband three years prior to her first son's birth, when she was eighteen and he was twenty-three. A sister, Fanny, had been born eighteen months earlier.

The family was not poor but neither was it well-off. John earned £176 a year, a substantial proportion of which was spent on house rent. He was not a lazy man and, by all accounts, he was a good father. He did not gamble, nor did he drink to excess. His problem, his weakness, however, was one he shared with Mr Wilkins Micawber in *David Copperfield*: he simply could not make ends meet, his expenditure regularly exceeding his income. This, as he and Mr Micawber both recognised, was a recipe for disaster.

'Annual income twenty pounds,' declares Micawber, like a Chancellor of the Exchequer lecturing the House of Commons, 'annual expenditure nineteen nineteen six, result happiness. Annual income twenty pounds, annual expenditure twenty pounds ought and six, result misery.'

If only modern economists could explain themselves so plainly. But while Dickens's father realised the misery that would follow from falling into debt he seemed utterly incapable of doing anything to prevent it. Instead he was someone who liked to act as if he had money to burn. He was the kind of man who would invite all and sundry to his house to enjoy lavish hospitality. In company he could not keep his hands out of his pocket. He was, as they say, generous to a fault.

It was not long after his son was born that his hope-lessness with money began to make itself felt. The modest house in which Dickens was born was beyond their means and the family moved to a smaller one. Nevertheless John's salary allowed him to employ a maid and his son's earliest recollections were happy. The outskirts of Portsmouth were pretty and rural and the town itself was bustling, full of sailors and soldiers readying themselves for war either with the Americans or the French.

Over the coming years the family increased in size. In 1816, Dickens acquired a baby sister, and his father was given a rise and a new post in the naval dockyard at Chatham, near the cathedral city of Rochester on the River Medway, to the east of the ever-growing city of London. John's annual salary was now £300 and, befitting a man who believed himself to be on the up, he rented a three-storey house and engaged two servants, one of whom fed Dickens's appetite for tales that were as gruesome as they were gripping. One, for example, involved a Captain Murderer who slaughtered wives as swiftly as he found them, baked them in pies, ate them and picked the bones. He got his comeuppance when one of his potential victims injected a pie with a poison which made him swell up like a balloon and turn blue until he filled the room from floor to ceiling and burst.

There were many more such tales which fascinated and horrified Dickens. He was, as authors often were, a sickly boy, prone, said his friend and biographer, John

Forster, to 'attacks of violent spasm which disabled him for any active exertion'. Games, even those that required little energetic involvement, by and large, were not for him. He preferred to observe from the sidelines, reading while others played.

It was his mother, who in his later years Dickens would occasionally disparage and claim had neglected him, who taught him to read. Like David Copperfield, Dickens saw reading as his 'only and. . . constant comfort. When I think of it, the picture always rises in my mind, of a summer evening, the boys at play in the churchyard, and I sitting on my bed, reading as if for life.'

What he read were classics, such as the novels of Tobias Smollett, including *Humphrey Clinker*, *Tom Jones* by Henry Fielding, Oliver Goldsmith's *The Vicar of Wakefield*, Cervantes's *Don Quixote* and Daniel Defoe's *Robinson Crusoe*, many of them concerned with travel and lands far beyond their reader's experience and knowledge.

'They kept alive my fancy,' Dickens later recalled, 'and my hope of something beyond that place and time – they, and the *Arabian Nights*, and the *Tales of the Genii* – and did me no harm'.

There is no better time to read than when young, when your taste is uninhibited and untainted and all you want to do is immerse yourself in a story. Books for Dickens were a form of escape. They were also populated by people whom he liked to impersonate. As one of his biographers has said, 'These fictional characters literally came alive to him; he could *see* them.' Thus he entered wholeheartedly into their lives, following them wherever they went, suffering when they suffered, rejoicing when they rejoiced.

Such engagement may seem odd and perhaps it was. What it did do, however, was blur in Dickens's young mind the distinction between fact and fiction, reality and dream. It is always wise to note that authors and the characters they create are usually not directly related. In Dickens's case, however, he often put much of himself into his characters, especially when they are young boys struggling to make headway in an unsympathetic world. Early on, it seems, Dickens came to realise that books could be his way out of a life that if he were not careful could consume and destroy him as he could see it was doing to so many others.

Like Oliver Twist, he wanted more. Like Oliver, too, he was inclined to self-pity and loneliness. 'He was alone in a strange place: and we all know how chilled and desolate the best of us will sometimes feel in such a situation,' Dickens wrote of Oliver, newly deposited in an undertaker's shop.

'The boy had no friends to care for, or to care for

him. The regret of no recent separation was
fresh in his mind; the absence of no loved and
remembered face sank heavily in his heart. But
his heart *was* heavy, notwithstanding; and he
wished, as he crept into his narrow bed, that
that were his coffin, and that he could be laid in
a calm and lasting sleep in the church-yard
ground, with the tall grass waving gently above
his head, and the sound of the old deep bell to
soothe him in his sleep.'

To a modern reader this may appear unduly morbid
but to Dickens and to his first readers it struck a chord
that was as familiar as it was resonant. For countless
children, the nineteenth century, a century of exhilarating
and frightening change, when Britain was transformed
in a few decades from a nation in which most of the
people lived and worked in the countryside to one in
which they were obliged to move to towns and cities and
work in factories, was a scary place. Growing up in
Chatham, Dickens must have sensed that such change
was on the way and drifting closer.

At sea, for instance, sail was being replaced by steam.
Where formerly the land had been tilled by hand
machines were increasingly in evidence. Small boys,
known as climbing boys, were required to climb up inside
chimneys taller than tenements in order to clean them.
Of course it was not something they were keen to do but
the alternatives were often worse.

'In what way were they forced up the chimneys?' a master sweep was asked during a government enquiry. 'By telling them we must take them back to their father and mother, and give them up again; and their parents are generally people who cannot maintain them.'

No facet of life remained unaltered. It was as if the entire world was being reinvented. Carriages pulled by horses were being replaced by trains. Goods were transported by canal. Mass production put paid to hand-made crafts. Soon everything would be available to everyone who could afford it. No family better encapsulates the new materialism than the nouveau riche Veneerings in *Our Mutual Friend*, one of Dickens' greatest novels. As their name suggests the Veneerings are embodied in their furniture.

> 'For in the Veneering establishment, from the hall-chairs with the new coat of arms, to the grand pianoforte with the new action, and upstairs again to the new fire-escape, all things were in a state of high varnish and polish. And what was observable in the furniture, was observable in the Veneerings – the surface smelt a little too much of the workshop and was a trifle sticky.'

No mention as yet has been made of schooling. In England and Wales compulsory education for children between five and twelve was not introduced until 1870 and even then many authorities did not consider it worthwhile. There were though many different types of schools to which children could be sent depending on family circumstances. Then as now there were the public schools such as Eton, which dates back to the mid-fifteenth century, and Rugby, which was founded a century and more later. But there was never any likelihood of Dickens attending either of these. His first school was what was known as a dame-school, so called because such establishments were run by elderly women. Expectations of them were not high, which was just as well. While it is true that the teachers could usually read and write their learning did not extend much further.

The school Dickens attended with his sister Fanny was above a dyer's shop and its memory lingered long for all the wrong reasons. The old woman who presided over it used a birch to control her charges. Later he modelled Mrs Pipchin in *Dombey and Son* on her, the kind of revenge only an author can exact. Mrs Pipchin, Dickens wrote, was an 'ogress' and a 'child-queller':

> '. . . a marvellous ill-favoured, ill-conditioned old lady, of a stooping figure, with a mottled face, like bad marble, a hook nose, and a hard grey eye, that looked as if it might have been hammered at on an anvil without sustaining any injury. . . She was generally spoken of as "a great manager" of children; and the secret of her management was, to give them everything they

didn't like, and nothing that they did – which
was found to sweeten their dispositions very
much.'

Dickens spent three years at this school before moving in 1821 to a bigger, and better, establishment, run by William Giles, a twenty-three-year-old Oxford graduate. Instantly, pupil and teacher got on famously and Dickens flourished in the enlightened atmosphere of learning. Boys, it was obvious, need not be thrashed to make them hard-working. If the dragon from the dame-school was to provide the prototype for one of Dickens's many monstrous teachers, William Giles was her counterpoint, a young, idealistic, kind and conscientious man who appears in a variety of guises throughout the novels as the personification of goodness and fairness. Under him Dickens studied enthusiastically and made swift progress.

But as if to emphasise that nothing good ever lasts the connection between the two was abruptly cut after just over a year. The cause of this wrench, as ever, was Dickens's father, whose financial troubles were now worse than ever. The family must move to London, Dickens was told, and their household goods must be sold off. To add insult to injury many of their effects were bought by a former servant girl. For reasons that remain unclear Dickens did not make the journey with his family but travelled later and alone.

On the night before he was due to leave Giles came to bid him farewell and presented him a copy of Oliver Goldsmith's *Bee*, which Dickens treasured for many years, representing as it doubtless did a symbol of a past which grew in hindsight to be far happier and freer than it truly was.

As the carriage rumbled along the road to London, rain poured ceaselessly. With no one to talk to, Dickens's thoughts turned gloomy, as did David Copperfield's:

> 'Through all the years that have since passed have I ever lost the smell of the damp straw in which I was packed – like game – and forwarded, carriage paid, to the Cross Keys, Wood Street, London?'

CHAPTER TWO
London

IN 1822, when Dickens's family arrived to make their home in it, London boasted a population of nearly a million and a half. Two decades before that it had stood at a million; eight decades later it was 4,500,000. Throughout the 1800s it grew faster than a mushroom cloud. People were pouring into it like rats into a sewer which, to a certain extent, is exactly what London was. They came from everywhere in search of streets paved with gold. Huge numbers of people arrived from rural Britain, sucked towards 'The Great Wen' by rampant unemployment and the very real fear of starvation. London was where dreams could be realised, pasts erased, hope ignited, selves reinvented.

It was the world's city, a bubbling melting pot of people drawn from near and far. It soon dwarfed all others. By the end of the nineteenth century its population was bigger than those of Scotland and Wales put together, bigger, too, than those of Australia and Switzerland, and twice those of Norway and Greece. Moreover, it was home to more Scots than Aberdeen, more Irish than Dublin, more Catholics than there were in Rome. Like Topsy it grew and grew and grew with little planning or foresight or consideration of the consequences. Nor is this surpris- ing. For this was an age in which the only constant was change. It was like living on a conveyor belt. Few had the opportunity or the desire to stand still and take stock. You either went with the flow or were drowned by it. As the century marched on every aspect of life, from the domestic to the political, religious to the scientific, would be radically altered. No age before or since has experienced such tumultuous upheaval.

Dickens's first impression of his new abode was far from favourable. While in later life he warmed to it and grew to love it, as a boy his view of the city with which his name has become synonymous was tainted by the fact of the reduced circumstances in which his family now found itself. 'The earliest impressions received by him in London were of his father's money involvements,' wrote John Forster.

The first sign that things were bad was the house in which they were to stay, which was in Bayham Street, Camden Town, one of the poorest parts of a city in which there was plenty of competition for that accolade. Dickens's room was in the garret where he wallowed in despair. All he could think about was the life he'd left behind in Chatham, including his old schoolmaster. 'What I would have given,' he recalled bitterly, 'if I had anything to give, to have been sent back to any other school, to have been taught something anywhere!'

His father's affairs were in a grim state and doubtless he passed on some of the stress this gave him to his wife and children. That Dickens should be sent to school was obviously not a high priority when keeping a roof over their heads and food on the table was a daily trial. Often, Dickens said, *very* often, there was not enough to eat. The butcher and the baker were among those clamouring at their door for payment. When none was forthcoming neither was food. Dickens felt sorry for himself and knew at whom to point the blame, but in hindsight he recognised that his father was essentially a good if flawed man.

When he was ill, Dickens remembered, his father would watch over him, mopping his brow and staying by his bedside until he got better. Moreover:

> 'He never undertook any business, charge or
> trust that he did not zealously, conscientiously,
> punctually, honourably discharge. His industry
> has always been untiring. He was proud of me,
> in his way. But, in the ease of his temper, and
> the straitness of his means, he appeared to have

lost at this time the idea of educating me at all,
and to have utterly put from him the notion that
I had any claim upon him, in that regard,
whatever.'

Why this affected Dickens so profoundly has never been fully explained. Except to suggest, of course, that even at this formative stage in his life he realised he was exceptional and that he needed to be educated to bring out in him the genius which he undoubtedly possessed. In his path stood his inept and feckless father. Dickens may have wanted to learn but this was a pipedream while the cupboard was bare and creditors hammered at the door.

That he was frustrated, angry, resentful, we must take as read. What made him even more upset was the fact that Fanny was getting an education and, what's more, doing well. A talented musician, she attended the Royal Academy of Music where she won prizes, to her brother's chagrin as he sat in the audience and watched her receive them.

'I could not bear to think of myself – beyond the reach of all such honourable emulation and success. The tears ran down my face. I prayed, when I went to bed that night, to be lifted out of the humiliation and neglect in which I was.'

Who knows what his father and mother made of such

hysteria. Or what they could have done to set it in context. Artists are notoriously fragile creatures, quick to assume slights and frequently and ferociously selfish and competitive. Dickens possessed all these characteristics and more. The American writer Gore Vidal once said that it was not enough for him to succeed; others must also fail. The same might be said of Dickens, who could not enthuse over his sister's success without feeling overcome with envy.

Everything, it appeared as his teens loomed, seemed to be stacked against him. But if ever he allowed himself to be lulled by the idea that things could not get any worse he was wrong: they were about to get very much worse. In order to raise some money for the family his mother found him a job through the good offices of James Lamert, a distant relative. Lamert was in charge of a blacking factory, Warren's, where it was agreed Dickens would be employed at a wage of six shillings a week. Thus, two days before he was twelve, began an experience which even later in his life, when his fame had spread across the globe and he was a wealthy and revered man, he talked about rarely and never without becoming emotional.

'It was a crazy, tumble-down old house,' was how he described his workplace near the Thames, 'abutting of course on the river, and literally overrun with rats. Its wainscotted rooms and its rotten floor and staircase, and the old grey rats swarming down in the cellars, and the sound of their scuffling coming up the stairs at all times, and the dirt and decay of the place, rise up visibly before me, as if I were there again.'

Warren's factory manufactured blacking for shoes. Dickens's task was:

> 'to cover the pots of paste-blacking; first with a piece of oilpaper, and then with a bit of blue paper; to tie them around with a string; and then to clip the paper close and neat, all round, until it looked as smart as a pot of ointment from an apothecary's shop.'

His day began at eight in the morning and ended at the same hour at night. One of his workmates was called Bob Fagin, whose surname he lent to the loathsome villain in *Oliver Twist* who leads a den of child pickpockets and who is ultimately hanged. Whether the real Fagin – who kindly took Dickens under his wing and showed him how to prepare his pots – deserved to be so remembered seems unlikely. Rather it was probably his misfortune that Dickens associated him with a period in his life that he would have preferred to forget. Having said that, there is little doubt that his spell in the blacking factory contributed to his development as a writer, rousing in him the need to publicise the conditions in which children were being used and abused.

There was certainly no lack of evidence. One need simply to browse through the pages of Henry Mayhew's *London Labour and the London Poor*, first published as a series of articles between 1850-2, to appreciate the extent to which children were treated as slaves who either did as their employers told them or were beaten and discarded, and left literally on the scrap heap. The problem was not a lack of work. It was its nature and the recompense it offered. There were bone-grubbers and rag-gatherers, dogs'-dung collectors and cigar-end finders, rat killers and hawkers of every hue. Scavenging was a full-time occupation. Everything, it seems, was recyclable and had its price, which was usually pitiful.

Even the sewers were treated as Aladdin's caves. 'There are a variety of perils to be encountered in such places,' remarked Mayhew. The walls could collapse, the rats were numerous, ferocious and had been known to attack men with 'fury', and when the tide came in the sewers often flooded. Drownings were common. One man, noted Mayhew, had been found near the mouth of the sewer 'quite dead, battered, and disfigured in a frightful manner.' Indeed the river itself, as Dickens described in *Our Mutual Friend*, was a ready and steady source of revenue, for there was money to be made by those prepared to fish corpses from its filthy water.

In such an unforgiving era, therefore, it was not inconceivable that even those who were relatively well off – which it must be accepted the Dickenses were – could fall from grace. This knowledge must have added to Charles's anxieties. Though he was contributing to the household's income in general the situation was decidedly bad. His father's affairs were now very bleak. Everything that could be pawned had been. The house was empty of furniture. There was nowhere to sleep or eat. All the books were gone. Nothing of value remained. With no means of placating those to whom he was in debt John Dickens was arrested and sent to the Marshalsea prison with no immediate prospect of release. Like his fellow inmates, he had little option but to remain in the prison until he could find the means to pay off those people he owed. But how could he do so while unable to earn enough to clear his debts? For such a proud man with an ambition to rise in society the shame must have been terrible.

The Marshalsea had long been a byword for hell. Its history can be traced back at least to the fourteenth century. In Elizabeth I's reign it was second in importance as a jail to the Tower of London, used mainly to house debtors. By the nineteenth century it was showing its age.

In *Little Dorrit*, the heroine is born in the prison, as many children were. It was, Dickens wrote in that novel, 'an oblong pile of barrack building, partitioned into squalid houses standing back to back, so that there were no back rooms; environed by a narrow paved yard, hemmed in by high walls duly spiked at top.'

In his preface to the novel Dickens did not allude to his own remembrance of the prison. In fact, he wrote, he did not know whether it was still standing until he got near to its end and paid its location a visit. Much, it seemed, had changed, but much had not. There was a great block of the former prison that he recognised though it had ceased to function as such. Enough, though, remained of it to make his memory of it vivid, standing as he did 'among the crowding ghosts of many miserable years'.

In total, John Dickens spent just fourteen weeks in the Marshalsea but it could have been a lifetime given the taint it left on him and his family. At the beginning he stayed there alone but as the weeks passed and there was no sign of anything – or anyone – turning up to rescue him he was joined by his wife and three youngest children. For the moment Fanny remained at the Royal Academy while Charles lodged with a friend of the family.

Charles grew increasingly resentful. In his eyes, he'd been cut adrift, abandoned, left to his own devices. He could have been an orphan for all that anyone cared. For someone so imaginative Dickens appears not to have sympathised with the plight of his parents and his siblings. What concerned him, what was uppermost in his mind, was the cruel neglect of himself.

> 'My own exclusive breakfast, of a penny cottage
> loaf and a pennyworth of milk, I provided for
> myself. I kept another small loaf, and a quarter
> pound of cheese, on a particular shelf of a
> particular cupboard: to make my supper when I
> came back at night. . . No advice, no counsel, no
> encouragement, no consolation, no support,
> from anyone that I can call to mind, so help me
> God.'

Who knows how accurate this account is. Dickens
himself was well aware that the passage of time plays
strange tricks.

'When my thoughts go back now to that slow agony of
my youth I wonder how much of the histories I invented
. . . hangs like a mist of fancy over well-remembered
facts!' he has David Copperfield say. 'When I tread the
old ground, I do not wonder that I seem to see and pity,
going on before me, an innocent, romantic boy, making
his imaginative world out of such strange experiences
and sordid things.'

Be that as it may, what is generally regarded as one of
the most grim periods in his life came to an abrupt end
when his father's mother died on 26th April, 1824 and
left her feckless son a bequest of £450. It would be some
time before his creditors were satisfied. But at least John
Dickens was free to leave the Marshalsea. He it was who

visited his son at the blacking factory and was appalled by the conditions in which he was working and ashamed that he had sanctioned it. As far as he was concerned Dickens must leave it straight away, which he was obviously keen to do. His mother, however, was appalled when she heard this news and argued that they could ill afford to lose the money Charles brought in. For the moment it looked as if there was to be no escape, he would be returned to his dank prison like a captured convict.

His mother, Dickens wrote later, was 'warm' for him being sent back. His father, however, was insistent. He would not allow it. He *could* not allow it. His son must leave the blacking factory, in which he had spent about four months, and go to school. And that was his final word on the matter.

CHAPTER THREE
School Years

ACCORDING to his former schoolmate, Owen P. Thomas, when Dickens entered Wellington House Academy as a twelve-year-old he was 'a healthy-looking boy, small but well-built, with a more than usual flow of spirits, inducing to harmless fun, seldom or ever I think to mischief, to which so many lads at that age are prone. I cannot recall anything that then indicated he would hereafter become a literary celebrity; but perhaps he was too young then.'

Dickens's initial reaction on joining his new school was surely one of relief. What he himself thought of the place was described by him in fact – in an essay titled 'Our School' – and in fiction in *David Copperfield*, where the school is called Salem House. Its headmaster and owner was a Welshman, William Jones, who was known for his ignorance and sadism.

It was rumoured that Jones, who it was believed had been in the leather trade, had bought the school from a proprietor who had been 'immensely learned', which may account for its inflated reputation. Of Jones, Dickens said:

> 'The only branches of education with which he
> showed the least acquaintance, were, ruling and
> corporally punishing. He was always ruling
> ciphering books with a bloated mahogany ruler,
> or smiting the palms of offenders with the same
> diabolical instrument, or viciously drawing a
> pair of pantaloons tight with one of his large
> hands, and caning the wearer with the other.
> We have no doubt whatever that this occupation
> was the principal solace of his existence.'

In *David Copperfield* Jones was transformed into Mr Creakle who delights 'in cutting at the boys, which was like the satisfaction of a craving appetite'. The school-room in which the cowed boys were taught offered no relief. It was the 'most forlorn and desolate place' with rows of desks and forms. The books were old and the dirty floor was littered with paper. More remarkably, there were two 'miserable' white mice which were kept in a castle made of pasteboard and wire. In a cage hopped a bird which never uttered a sound.

'There is,' observes Copperfield, 'a strange unwhole-some smell upon the room, like mildewed corduroys, sweet apples wanting air, and rotten books. There could not have been more ink splashed about it, if it had been roofless from its first construction, and the skies had rained, snowed, hailed, and blown ink through the vary-ing seasons of the year.'

This was where Dickens was to be a student for the next two and a half years. There were a few compens-ations. The first was that he did not board; at the end of each day he went home, which may have saved him from more severe punishment. Secondly, Jones employed several teachers who were actually capable of imparting knowledge. One taught mathematics and English while another specialised in Latin, for which Dickens won a prize.

The object of the school, however, was not learning. Rather its students were seen as customers and the more of them there were the greater the profit the owner could hope to make. It was, as so many schools at the time were, a money-making venture. Indeed, Dickens's mother had attempted to improve her family's finances by founding a school but it was stillborn and never, at least in Dickens's memory, attracted a single student.

As was his habit, Dickens's recollection of his time at Wellington House was diluted with humour. The school, he said, was rather famous for its 'mysterious pupils'. One boy had persuaded himself that he was the son of a viscount who had deserted his mother. 'It was understood that if he had his rights, he would be worth twenty thousand a year. And that if his mother ever met his father, she would shoot him with a silver pistol, which she carried, always loaded, for that purpose.' Another boy was said to carry a dagger 'about him somewhere'. None, though, could compare with the boy who claimed to have been born on the 29th of February, and to have a birthday every five years. 'We suspected this to have been a fiction – but he lived upon it all the time he was at Our School.'

Dickens himself appears to have been a normal, mischievous schoolboy. Wandering the streets with his friends he invented a language in the hope that those overhearing it would take its speakers to be foreigners. Once he persuaded his friends to pretend to be beggars and confronted old ladies asking for help. He wrote bad jokes for the school magazine and read what were known as penny dreadfuls, such as *The Terrific Register*, which scared him witless but nevertheless gave him a taste for the macabre.

Reading was the rage of the age and was seen as the way to improve oneself; the more you read the better informed and better equipped you were to get on. The self-educated reader was as much a product of the times as was the self-educated writer. There were no free public libraries as we know them today. They would not become common until towards the end of the century. You could either pay to use circulating libraries or buy books which, in the early decades of the 1800s, were prohibitively expensive and regarded as luxury items. A house in which there were many books was one whose owners were assumed to be wealthy and educated.

But by the end of the 1820s the price of books began to tumble and, almost overnight, they were affordable to all but the poorest in society. This came about because a few publishers decided to publish well-known books in cheap editions. One such was Thomas Cadell who, in the summer of 1829, having acquired the copyright of Sir Walter Scott's works, began to issue them at five shillings a volume. Less than two years later another enterprising publisher, Colburn and Bentley, began to publish its series of Standard Novels, some priced at a third of what they had cost previously. The discounting worked and the market expanded elastically.

'Suddenly – and belatedly – the prosperous artisan or clerk with a few shillings to spend loomed more important than the gentleman with a guinea or two,' wrote Richard D. Altick in *The English Common Reader*. It was, he added, Britain's 'first great cheap-literature craze'. Soon, where books had led, magazines and news-papers followed, catering for every taste high and low.

Print was what the masses craved and there was a plentiful supply.

Dickens left his schooldays behind in May 1827. He was short for his years and looked younger. There was, of course, never any suggestion that he would attend university, even though his family's fortunes had improved. On his retirement from the Navy his father had been given a pension which he supplemented with working as a journalist in the House of Commons.

Ends were being met but the household budget was still tight. So Dickens started out as an office boy in a law firm, Ellis and Blackmore, where he was taken on at ten shillings a week. It was not the kind of job which encouraged him to leap out of bed of a morning but, as ever with Dickens, it was not forgotten when he turned his hand to literature. Mr Ellis, the firm's senior partner, is surely the model for Mr Perker in *The Pickwick Papers*, who is routinely described as 'little' and is a habitual user of snuff.

Dickens was no more than a dogsbody, fetching and carrying documents. Had he stuck at it he may well have advanced to become a solicitor or a judge but that was too distant a prospect for him. Patience was never one of his virtues and he wanted to rise much more quickly in the world. For once, it seems, his father was the example he chose to follow.

Like him, Dickens saw journalism as a way of making a decent living. The key was to learn shorthand, which John Dickens had done. This, in turn, led to him joining the elite Parliamentary corps of journalists whose members could earn about fifteen guineas a week when the Palace of Westminster was in session. To Dickens this was a huge sum of money. Moreover, many men who had begun as reporters in the House of Commons had gone on to distinguish themselves in other walks of life.

First, however, he put his skills to use in the courts, taking down notes and evidence. It was tedious work which called for accuracy and concentration. On the plus side it offered Dickens a ringside seat in a theatre through which all human life passed. Often cases proceeded at a pace that would make snails look like Olympic sprinters. Writing much later Dickens cited one such that had been going on for nearly twenty years, involving numerous lawyers and costing in the region of £70,000, an astronomical sum for the time. And this, noted Dickens, is '*a friendly suit*'. Nor was it anywhere near a conclusion. Not that this was unusual. Another suit had lasted more than a half century and so far costs had swallowed up in excess of £140,000.

'If I wanted other authorities for JARNDYCE AND JARNDYCE,' remarked Dickens, in his preface to *Bleak House*, the novel in which that infamous, never-ending case features, 'I could rain them on these pages.'

It must have seemed to Dickens that he too was destined to spend his life trapped in a courtroom watching the wheels of justice turn ever more slowly. His determination was to move on but as yet an opportunity had not presented itself.

In the meantime he did what he could to supplement his education. In February 1830 he applied for a reader's ticket at the British Museum which gave him access to a library of around a quarter of a million books. For the next three years Dickens read as if making up for lost time. These were, he reflected, the most useful years of his life, which the records confirm. Among the many books he read were the plays of Shakespeare, the essays of Joseph Addison and Richard Steele and Oliver Goldsmith's *History of England*.

For amusement, and perhaps with an eye to a future career, he was also a regular attender at the theatre, one of his lifelong passions. In his early life he was taken by relatives and revelled in pantomime. He was particularly impressed with the performances of Joseph Grimaldi, the legendary clown, whose memoirs Dickens edited a year after his death in 1837. Pantomime, Dickens said, was:

> 'that jocund world. . . where there is no affliction or calamity that leaves the least impression. . . where everyone, in short, is so superior to all

the accidents of life, though encountering them
at every turn.'

It was a brutal, unsentimental world in which comedy
and tragedy clashed. Nothing amused the adult Dickens
more than to play the clown. Once, he was capering on
the edge of a bath and fell into the water.

The truth is he loved to perform as he much as he
loved performers. Whenever he could he would improvise
and act, to such an extent that when writing his novels
he would play out scenes in front of a mirror before
committing them to paper. His public readings were *tours
de force*, in which he adopted roles, gave voice to different
characters and ran the gamut of emotions. Audiences,
he was not too immodest to record, loved it, laughing at
the entrance of a comic character, and weeping uncon-
trollably at the departure of others.

Most modern novelists might find this kind of
posturing and the reaction it provoked embarrassing.
Not Dickens. He revelled in it and the celebrity that
accompanied it. Were there such people as paparazzi he
would have happily posed for them. When he was
stopped in the street by a woman and complimented for
filling her house with many friends he was touched.

All of that, though, was some years in the future. Aged
18, he did for the first time what young men tend to do;
he fell in love. The object of his desire was Maria

Beadnell, the daughter of a banker, who was fifteen months older than he was. By all accounts she was a bright-eyed beauty with 'bewitching' curls. The exact nature of their relationship is unknown. That Dickens loved her there seems no doubt. Whether this was reciprocated is another matter.

In search of Dickens's true feelings scholars return to David Copperfield and his passion for Dora Spenlow:

> 'She was more than human to me. She was a Fairy, a sylph, I don't know what she was – anything that no one ever saw, and everything that everybody ever wanted. I was swallowed up in an abyss of love in an instant'.

For three years Dickens pursued Maria until she finally told him she no longer wanted to see him. The pain was intense as rejection always was for Dickens. Two decades later it returned with interest when, now married and a mother, she wrote to him out of the blue. In reply, he asked if she'd read *David Copperfield* which, he said, contained:

> 'a faithful reflection of the passion I had for you, and in little bits of 'Dora' touches of your old self sometimes and a grace here and there that may be revived in your little girls. . . People used to say to me how pretty all that was, and how fanciful it was, and how elevated it was above the little foolish loves of very young men and

women. But they little thought what reason I had
to know it was true and nothing more or less.'

Fruitless as it eventually proved, Dickens's pursuit of
Maria was another spur for him to improve himself. And
at last opportunity knocked. In 1828 his uncle John
Barrow has started the *Mirror of Parliament*, a publication that was devoted to keeping a verbatim record of
Parliamentary proceedings. Four years later Dickens was
taken on its staff and soon thereafter he was also made
a reporter on a new evening newspaper called the *True
Sun*. It was not long before he made his mark. Or, as he
put it, he made 'a great splash'. Nor was this only his
opinion. One hardened parliamentary hack said: 'There
never *was* such a shorthand writer!' His speed and, more
importantly, his accuracy soon became legendary and
his earnings rose accordingly. Working overtime he could
make as much as twenty-five guineas a week. Still just
twenty years of age Dickens had taken his first significant
steps on the ladder that would lead him to the dizzy
heights of success.

CHAPTER FOUR
Mr Pickwick

WRITING is the most ecologically correct way of making a living. Nothing goes to waste, everything is recyclable. From the moment a writer is born until he draws his last breath he is a human vacuum cleaner, sucking up whatever he sees and hears, feels and thinks, never knowing when it all might be useful, never knowing when it will materialise as words on a page.

The early years are crucial. Take any major writer. Their childhood is what distinguishes them. Some are scarred by it and would rather it was forgotten; others look back upon it as a magical time impossible to retrieve. Either way they are haunted by memories embedded in their upbringing. But for every writer there comes a moment when they make the transition from consumer to producer, when they cease simply to be a reader and they become a writer. For Dickens this bridge was crossed in 1832 when he wrote a fictional sketch called 'A Dinner at Poplar Walk', which was published in *The Monthly Magazine*.

No one should ever underestimate what it feels like to see one's work in print for the first time. Dickens was no exception. Later he recalled buying the magazine at a bookshop on the Strand and, overwhelmed with emotion, he hurriedly made his way across the teeming city, desperate to be alone in order to savour the moment, his eyes 'dimmed with pride and joy'. He was just twenty years of age and already a *bona fide* author.

Four years later he published his first book, *Sketches by Boz*, and fame and fortune beckoned. Almost overnight Dickens went from obscurity to someone whose name was known everywhere.

He chose to give himself the pseudonym 'Boz' not because he was ashamed of his own name but because it was intriguing. It was, he related long after he'd revealed himself to be the author of the sketches, the nickname of a younger brother whom he'd dubbed Moses which, when said through his nose, became Boses, which was shortened to Boz. It was, moreover, an age when nicknames were popular. For example, Hablot Knight

Browne, who provided a number of illustrations for the book, was known as 'Phiz'. Who Boz was, however, was not truly much of a mystery. Everyone who was anyone knew that he and Dickens were one.

In *Sketches by Boz* Dickens immersed himself in whatever took his fancy, which was just about everything. Curiosity is a trait every writer must have and Dickens had it in spades. He was, as the writer Christopher Isherwood remarked of himself, a camera with his shutter open. Open any page of *Sketches by Boz* and you find a writer revelling in his surroundings, alive to every sensation, interested in anything that moved. In one of the sketches he described taking an early morning walk through London's streets, evoking hour by hour the Great Wen coming awake.

'The last drunken man,' wrote Dickens, 'who shall find his way home before sunlight, has just staggered heavily along, roaring out the burden of the drinking song of the previous night: the last houseless vagrant whom penury and police have left in the streets, has coiled up his chilly limbs in some paved corner, to dream of food and warmth. The drunken, the dissipated, and the wretched have disappeared; the more sober and orderly part of the population have not yet awakened to the labours of the day, and the stillness of death is over the streets; its very hue seems to be imparted to them, cold and lifeless as they look in the grey, sombre light of daybreak. The coach-stands in the larger thoroughfares are deserted; the night-houses are closed; and the chosen promenades of profligate misery are empty.'

Sketches by Boz is full of such passages, many of which dwell on the enormous changes that were sweeping city and country. It was both good and bad as Dickens was all too aware. While many people prospered it was often at the expense of others. Dickens watched in wonder, reporting what he saw but colouring it with personal experience.

While a naturally humorous writer he knew, too, the value of pathos. Comedy is to be found in tragedy and *vice-versa*. London, whose paths many really did believe were paved with gold, was a magnet to the masses intent on self-improvement. The city offered not only employment but also sanctuary. It was a place in which to realise oneself, to be whoever you wanted to be.

As a young man Dickens liked nothing better than to wander around it, even at night, when the crowds had disappeared and the noise and bustle were replaced by those, such as Lizzie and her father in *Our Mutual Friend* who make their living by fishing bodies out of the River Thames. Indeed, soon, as Dickens grew ever more famous and his face more and more recognisable, it was only at night when he could walk the capital's streets undisturbed.

Shortly after the appearance of *Sketches by Boz* Dickens was asked by a publisher to write a serial in twenty instalments. It was an offer that was as tempting as it was irresistible. It also presented a considerable challenge. With an inflexible deadline, Dickens had to produce 12,000 words a month, in addition to whatever other work he had agreed to do. However, the reward made refusal unthinkable: he would make about £14 a month which, he calculated, would allow him to marry Catherine.

And so *The Pickwick Papers* came into being. Its author, it's worth underlining, was still young, just 24, still feeling his way as a writer. As one critic has written, 'The book was probably written more from hand to mouth than those which followed it, with the author scarcely knowing from number to number what he was going to do with his characters or his characters were going to do with him.'

This was surely true. In hindsight, Dickens himself said that the book began with Mr Pickwick and grew from there, as is often the way with writers. He called him in the first paragraph 'immortal' and so he has become. After an uncertain start – early sales of the serial were poor and there were problems with the illustrations – Pickwick captured the public's imagination. By the fourth instalment, when Mr Pickwick encounters Sam Weller cleaning shoes in the White Hart Yard and offers him a job, sales began to pick up. What a month or so previously had been a trickle grew to a gush and then to a flood. Chapman and Hall, the publisher, printed more and more copies in order to meet demand and, mindful of Dickens's rising star, upped their monthly payment to £25. By the time the serialisation drew to a close 40,000 copies were being printed.

Everyone who could read it and those couldn't read had it read to them. All, irrespective of their station in life, were charmed by the guileless Mr Pickwick, who is tricked again and again by scoundrels yet always retains our sympathy and respect. Like Don Quixote, he is an innocent abroad in a world that views men like him as an easy touch. Yet while we fear for him we never sneer at him. For here was described an England that had much appeal, where eccentricity flourished and kindness was common. Amusement was uppermost in the minds of Mr Pickwick and his chums. Tell them there was a game of cricket to be played and they would abandon everything to take part. And when not playing, it seemed, they were eating. It's been estimated that in *The Pickwick Papers* there are approximately 35 breakfasts, 32 dinners and 10 luncheons. Moreover few hours passed without a drink.

'There was a vast deal of deal of talking and rattling of knives and forks, and plates: a great running about of three ponderous head waiters, and a rapid disappearance of the substantial viands on the table,' wrote Dickens of one memorable Pickwickian dinner. 'When everybody had eaten as much as possible, the cloth was removed, bottles, glasses, and dessert were placed on the table; and the waiters withdrew to "clear away", or in other words, to appropriate to their own private use and emolument whatever remnants of the eatables and drinkables they could contrive to lay their hands on.'

Dickens instinctively knew what his readers wanted. As they read such passages their lips would literally be licking while their stomachs rumbled like distant thunder. It has been said that Dickens wrote so much about food and drink because he had often gone hungry in his youth. That may well be the case. One recalls, for example, the lovingly described Christmas dinner in *Great Expectations*, including 'a leg of pickled pork and greens, and a pair of roast stuffed fowls' all swimming in gravy. Then there were mince pies, brandy, gin, pudding, nuts and oranges and apples, and, to cap it all, a savoury pork pie.

This was the kind of meal over which many people fantasised. It was also the kind of meal many could ill afford. Not long after Dickens wrote *The Pickwick Papers* it was calculated that a grown man could be kept 'in health and fit for labour' on a pound and a half of 'good' bread a day. If this were washed down with a quart of milk it was believed that he could keep himself for eight or nine days with half a crown, which is 25p in today's money. Few, however, actually earned this much and many earned much less. Of course, money in the mid-nineteenth century went much further than it does now but even allowing for this it is clear that poverty was general and unignorable, especially by someone with Dickens's sensitivity. We must beware, however, of judging earlier generations by the values of our own.

One of the most remarkable features of the Victorian era (which began in 1838 when Queen Victoria was crowned) was the uncomplaining nature of the English masses. Conditions that to us appear brutal, degrading and unbearable were often accepted uncomplainingly, as if, in fact, they were normal. 'There is,' remarked one social commentator, 'a sense of patient resignation to the facts of life, the feeling that human existence is a struggle and that survival is an end in itself. Especially is this so in relation to the early death of wives or children – a fatalistic attitude that "God gives and God takes away", and that although one may mourn, one does not inveigh against the Fates which, to us, seem to have treated some so cruelly.'

In time, as his career progressed and his influence grew, Dickens was to prove the most eloquent and persuasive critic of a society that allowed such attitudes to become ingrained. There was, it's worth bearing in mind, no real democracy in England until much later in the nineteenth century. Thus the poor and disenfranchised had little option but to accept their lot. Enlightenment and improvement came about slowly and invariably because of the interference of those like Dickens who could not tolerate how other human beings were forced to live.

Dickens's means of doing this was through fiction, beginning with what's been termed his 'first attempt at a proper novel', namely *Oliver Twist*. It's a story that is as familiar as it is evergreen. Oliver, like Huckleberry Finn, like Jim Hawkins in *Treasure Island*, is a boy alone in the world. The picture that for many readers sums up the novel is that of Oliver in the workhouse, driven by hunger, to ask for more food.

This, Dickens relates, was the result of 'slow starvation' over three months. Oliver, his starved fellows have decided, should be the one to make the request. 'Please, sir, I want some more,' he says to the master, Mr Bumble. It does not, alas, get the desired response. First, he is hit with a ladle then he is reported to 'the board', whose chairman, Mr Limbkins, cannot believe what he is hearing. Finally, he says:

> 'Compose yourself, Bumble, and answer me
> distinctly. Do I understand that he asked for
> more, after he had eaten the supper allotted by
> the dietary?'
> 'He did, sir,' replies Bumble.

To which Mr Limbkins says:
'That boy will be hung. I know that boy will be hung.'

What Dickens set out to do in *Oliver Twist* was hold up a mirror to a society that was so sick it was no longer able to recognise itself. While empires were being built and factories were running throughout the night, the effect on ordinary people was largely ignored. Children in particular were the victims of such rampant industry. Oliver, who nearly dies before he takes his first breath, is an orphan, 'badged and ticketed. . . despised by all, and pitied by none'. After running away from those who see in his future a noose around his neck he falls in with Fagin and his gang of child pickpockets and appears set on becoming a criminal, like so many of his contemporaries.

What Dickens hoped to show in *Oliver Twist* was that crime was a sordid and squalid and reprehensible way to make one's living. This was in contrast to other depictions of thieves which often had the reverse effect.

'In every book I know,' wrote Dickens in the novel's preface, 'where such characters are treated of, allurements and fascinations are thrown around them. Even in *The Beggar's Opera* [by John Gay], the thieves are represented as leading a life which is rather to be envied than otherwise. . .'

Having said which, Oliver was the example, albeit a rare one, which disproved the rule. But he was redeemed for the sake of the fiction rather than the need to reflect life as it really was. Dickens may have been concerned with the social fabric of the country but his prime aim was to write a book that gripped and amused people. In that regard he was, like most great writers, possessed of a splinter of ice in his heart.

Oliver Twist, he assessed once it was written, was a 'marvellous tale'. And the public agreed. It was read by everyone, from duchesses to thieves, adding, ironically, to Dickens's burgeoning wealth. In 1869, a year before his death, Dickens resurrected *Oliver Twist*, personally presenting to audiences a dramatisation of the murder of Nancy, the prostitute who works for Fagin, by Bill Sikes, the evil burglar. Dickens impersonated them all, becoming the characters he had himself created, bringing them to life on the stage as he had done on the page. It was as if he couldn't let go of them, as if they were alive.

'Gradually warming with excitement he flung aside the book,' recalled one witness, 'and acted the scene of the murder, shrieked the terrified pleadings of the girl, growled the brutal savagery of the murderer. . . The raised hands, the bent-back head, are good; but shut your eyes and the illusion is more complete. The cries for mercy, the Bill! dear Bill! for God's sake! uttered in tones in which the agony of fear prevails even over the earnestness of the prayers, the dead dull voice as hope departs, are intensely real. When the pleading ceases, you open your eyes in relief, in time to see the impersonation of the murderer seizing a heavy club and striking his victim to the ground.'

CHAPTER FIVE

Dotheboys Hall

IF biographers of Dickens are agreed on one thing it is that he was a man of many parts. He had, it seems, a wonderful capacity for compartmentalisation. When working on a book, he knuckled down, occasionally removing himself from his family and routine to places where he knew he would not be disturbed. In the main, though, he combined writing with a variety of other activities, some domestic, some social, some profess-ional. But wherever he went and whatever he did he was the centre of attraction, holding the floor, directing the action, a volcano emitting ideas. Life as he saw it was too fragile to waste doing nothing.

Like Balzac, his French counterpart, he was intent on

creating a world and populating it with characters who spoke distinctively. Many writers today are happy to have all their characters speak similarly, often leaving it to readers to improvise accents. This would not have done for Dickens who liked to hear his characters speak even as he was finding the right words for them.

In that sense, he was a mimic and an accomplished one. Nothing was left to chance. He wanted his readers not only to see his characters but also to hear them, the better to bring them into being. Invariably, before his books were published, he read them aloud to family and friends, partly because it pleased him to do so and partly to gauge their reaction.

No author worked harder than Dickens did to give his readers what they wanted. But it would be too glib to dismiss him as a mere crowd pleaser. In novel after novel he proved himself to be an innovator who, having built his fan club, was able to carry it with him on any journey he chose to take.

Oliver Twist, though very different from *The Pickwick Papers*, confirmed and consolidated Dickens's position as England's most popular novelist. Even as he was finishing it, however, he had begun to contemplate a new and much more ambitious work. This was what would become *Nicholas Nickleby*. It was sparked by press reports of a Yorkshire schoolmaster, one William Shaw, who kept an academy at Bowes, near Greta Bridge, on the bleak North Yorkshire moors. Shaw was sued for negligence by the parents of two children who became blind because of lack of medical treatment for an infection. Though convicted and ordered to pay damages of £500, he continued to run his school. The churchyard at Bowes has the graves of twenty-five boys, aged from seven to eighteen who died there between 1810 and 1834.

For obvious and painful reasons education was a subject close to Dickens's heart. In the preface to *Nicholas Nickleby* he expressed exactly what he thought of it in his day. He was not complimentary:

> 'Of the monstrous neglect of education in England, and the disregard of it by the State as a means of forming good or bad citizens, and miserable or happy men, private schools long afforded a notable example. Although any man who had proved his unfitness for any other occupation in life, was free, without examination or qualification, to open a school anywhere; although preparation for the functions he undertook, was required in the surgeon who assisted to bring a boy into the world, or might one day assist, perhaps, to send him out of it; in the chemist, the attorney, the butcher, the baker, the candlestick maker; the whole round of crafts and trades, the schoolmaster excepted; and although schoolmasters, as a race, were the blockheads and impostors who might naturally be expected to spring from such a state of

things, and to flourish in it; these Yorkshire schoolmasters were the lowest and most rotten round the whole ladder. Traders in the avarice, indifference, or imbecility of parents, and the helplessness of children; ignorant, sordid, brutal men, to whom few considerate persons would have entrusted the board and lodging of a horse or a dog; they formed the worthy cornerstone of a structure, which, for absurdity and a magnificent high-minded *laissez-faire* neglect, has rarely been exceeded in the world.'

Reform was slow in coming. For example, it was not until 1870 that an Act of Parliament was introduced to establish a proper system of elementary schools in England and Wales. Locally elected boards were to provide schools where there were deficiencies. This Act was the beginning of the so-called 'dual system' which still exists in the twenty-first century, whereby schools funded by the state exist alongside commercially run private schools known, confusingly, as 'public' schools. In 1880, it was made compulsory for children to be educated to ten years of age. In 1918, this was raised to 14, and in 1973 to 16.

But while entry to the teaching profession was increasingly strictly controlled in the state sector this was not always so in public schools. Here standards varied widely well into the twentieth century, offering many novelists with firsthand experience of the profession plenty of scope for satire. One such was Evelyn Waugh who, in his novel *Decline and Fall*, first published in 1928, had his hero, Paul Pennyfeather, seek employment in a public school despite having no previous experience and having been sent down from Oxford because of indecent behaviour. When told this the headmaster of Llanabba Castle says: 'Indeed, indeed? Well, I shall not ask for details. I have been in the scholastic profession long enough to know that nobody enters it unless he has some very good reason which he is anxious to conceal.'

It was the kind of reaction that would not have surprised Dickens. Fuelled by outrage and scenting the germ of a story, he travelled with his illustrator, Hablot Browne, from London to Yorkshire. In order to avoid suspicion he took an assumed name. He also pretended that he had been asked by a recently widowed mother to find a school for her son. To that end he carried a letter of introduction to a schoolmaster. It was January, gnawingly cold and snowing heavily. Coach trips always gave Dickens a plentiful supply of colour and this one was no different. On board was a Yorkshire school-mistress who drank brandy until she was unconscious. When awake she told Dickens that she too was carrying a letter, from a father wanting to know why his son wouldn't eat boiled meat.

Over the course of a few wintry days Dickens visited

several places on and around the moors. There were, it seemed, many schools in the area eager for business. Eventually he met one of the schoolmasters he was so eager to quiz, plying him with drink in the hope of loosening his tongue.

' "Was there any large school near?" I asked him.

"Oh yes," he said; "there was a pratty big 'un."

"Was it a good one?" I asked.

"Ey!" he said, "It was as good as anoother; that was a' a matter of opinion"; and fell to looking at the fire, staring round the room, and whistling a little. On my reverting to some other topic that we had been discussing, he recovered immediately; but, though I tried him again and again, I never approached the question of the school, even if he were in the middle of a laugh, without observing that his countenance fell, and that he became uncomfortable.'

It is clear from what Dickens himself recalled of his Yorkshire jaunt that in terms of research it was not as fruitful as he might have hoped. He had, however, seen for himself the surroundings in which the schools were located and he did have a brief if unsatisfactory encounter with William Shaw, whose case had first got him interested in the schools and who was understandably reluctant to volunteer information.

But Dickens had seen enough to know exactly where and to what he was sending Nicholas Nickleby. Like the school run by Shaw, Dotheboys Hall is situated near Greta Bridge. Here, boasted its master, Wackford Squeers, at the 'delightful' village of Dotheboys, boys were 'boarded, clothed, booked, washed, furnished with pocket-money, provided with all necessaries. . .'

Squeers, as indeed are his wife and daughter, is a comic grotesque, the kind of man you would never want to meet except in the pages of a book. In Dickens's hands he became a byword for monstrously cruel and ignorant schoolmasters, his only motive money, his sole skill whipping boys within an inch of their lives. The Squeers are greedy and fat, in contrast to their pupils who, when first seen by Nicholas, appear as undernourished and abused as survivors in a concentration camp.

'There were little faces which should have been hand-some,' wrote Dickens, 'darkened with the scowl of sullen, dogged suffering; there was childhood with the light of its eye quenched, its beauty gone, and its helplessness alone remaining; there were vicious-faced boys, brooding, with leaden eyes, like malefactors in a jail; and there were young creatures on whom the sins of their frail parents had descended, weeping even for the mercenary nurses they had known, and lonesome even in their loneliness. With every kindly sympathy and affection blasted in its birth, with every young and healthy feeling flogged and starved down, with every vengeful passion that can fester in swollen hearts eating its evil way to their core in silence, what an incipient Hell was breeding here!'

Some readers may think that in such passages Dickens is guilty of exaggeration. But given what we know about the Yorkshire schools and their treatment of their pupils the opposite is more likely to be true. What we do know for certain is that his portrayal of Squeers was so eerily accurate that several schoolmasters, including Shaw, threatened to sue Dickens, which is an ironic testimony of his accuracy. We also know that Shaw's school was in no sense Dotheboys Hall's inferior when it came to inflicting pain and distress. One boy, who was blinded there, recalled: 'five boys generally slept in a bed. . . On a Sunday they had pot skimmings for tea, in which there was vermin. . . there were eighteen boys there beside himself, of whom two were totally blind.'

The public response to *Nicholas Nickleby* was nothing less than phenomenal. As usual it was originally published in monthly parts, the first of which sold over 50,000 copies. Though there was much about it that was tragic this was leavened by swathes of pure comedy.

Instinctively, Dickens knew that he needed to make his readers laugh through their tears. It was as if *The*

Pickwick Papers and *Oliver Twist* had mated. As one critic said, *Nicholas Nickleby* mingles the sunlight of *Pickwick Papers* with the darkness of *Oliver Twist*.

Meanwhile parents withdrew their sons in droves from the schools and the schools rapidly closed down. Dickens himself noted that when he began to write his novel there were a 'good many cheap Yorkshire schools in existence'. By the time he got round to penning his preface that number had been drastically reduced. It was proof, were it needed, of the power of storytelling, that the pen, when wielded by genius, could be mightier than the sword.

Nor was Dickens unaware of his own growing influence on affairs. In some quarters he was regarded as the conscience of England, the one person who could be relied upon to speak out, who would not be silenced. Where formerly he had to struggle to make ends meet, he was now invited into the homes of the gentry, where he was praised and patronised in equal measure. If the latter hurt him he could always turn it to his advantage, for satirists always have the last word. One evening he might be dining with the great and the good while the following day he would be taken on a tour of factories where he would be disgusted and astonished by the conditions in which people worked.

'I mean to strike the heaviest blow for these unfortunate creatures,' he wrote after one such visit.

And eventually he would. But that was far in the future. For the moment, though, Dickens was prey to his passions. Even as he was completing *Nicholas Nickleby* he had an idea for a weekly magazine. It was, he decreed, to be called *Master Humphrey's Clock*, which was not the snappiest of titles. He wanted to produce a publication that would be amusing, that would contribute to its readers' happiness. It would also, Dickens reckoned, make him happy, by providing him with a steady income and a share in any profits.

Clearly, he was not unaware of his own worth. He knew that others profited from his talent and labour and he wanted to ensure that he got his fair share. Apart from anything else he had a growing family to maintain, aged parents to look after, siblings to keep an eye on. The more successful he became the more tangled were his business dealings. Contracts were disputed. Who had the rights to which books? What had Dickens promised to do? Had he met his obligations? Quite often he was at loggerheads with his publishers. Financial wrangling consumed too much of his precious time. Lawyers poked their expensive noses in. Dickens was convinced he was right as were those opposing him.

All of which is part of a writer's life. The relationship between a writer and his publisher is key. Read any major writer's biography and a large portion of it will be devoted to his publisher. Few of these pages are without trouble.

As Dickens was only too aware, a generation earlier Sir Walter Scott, the first writer to merit the label 'bestselling', was ruined because of the reckless actions of his publisher. Indeed, it was around this time that he visited Scott's home at Abbotsford in the Scottish borders.

In so many ways Scott and Dickens were alike. Both, for instance, had started their careers by writing under pseudonyms. Both, too, had become famous and wealthy by their pens. Like Scott, Dickens worked all hours, rarely resting. When the two men did leave their desks they walked and walked, Scott in the country, Dickens in the city. Abbotsford, as Dickens appreciated, was a monument to Scott's energy and folly, a place that was at once magnificent and ridiculous, a home that looked like a museum, with its collection of arms and armour and bric-a-brac.

Dickens was moved and appalled. Here was Scott's 'old white hat, which seemed to be tumbled and bent and broken by the uneasy, purposeless wandering hither and thither of his heavy head'. Scott, he realised, had driven himself to the grave writing to pay off debts. He never 'left off', never finished one project without having another ready to start. There was no respite, no time to take stock, no chance for him to replenish his energy. Dickens was chastened but dare he listen to his own heart? Dare he lay aside his pen even for a few months and put up his feet?

CHAPTER SIX
Little Nell's Death

THE cruellest and wisest thing Dickens ever did was to allow Little Nell to die. In the eyes of many readers, many of whom were his most devoted fans, it made him nothing less than a murderer. It is, of course, entirely up to an author whether one of his characters lives or dies. Arthur Conan Doyle, for example, sent Sherlock Holmes over the Reichenbach Falls, seemingly to his death. His readers were appalled and implored Doyle to revive him which he did, albeit reluctantly. More recently, J.K. Rowling, author of the *Harry Potter* series, let it be known that she intended killing off one of her characters, which prompted many of her readers to plead for their favourites to be spared. Their prayers went unanswered.

Little Nell is the heroine of *The Old Curiosity Shop*, Dickens's fifth book. The author described it as 'the little child-story' and it began life, in 1840, as an article for his new weekly magazine, *Master Humphrey's Clock*, in which he hoped that characters would keep reappearing, as at a club or in a soap opera. Little Nell's story was one among many that Dickens planned would be told by Master Humphrey. What he had not planned, however, was the grip Little Nell would take of his imagination and that of the reading public. The first part of *The Old Curiosity Shop* appeared in the fourth issue of the magazine. By the time it reached its tragic conclusion, in February 1841 after forty episodes, sales had peaked at 100,000, and Little Nell's name was known throughout the English-speaking world.

When first we meet her Little Nell is lost, literally and metaphorically, wandering the streets of London in the dark, and subject to who knows what danger. Like his creator, the narrator Master Humphrey likes to walk at night, 'because it affords me greater opportunities of speculating on the characters and occupations of those who fill the streets'. One night he finds Nell at his side who tells him that she is frightened and doesn't know her way home. Master Humphrey is impressed by the trust she puts in him but when he asks what she has been doing, she replies: 'That, I must not tell.'

It is the tantalising beginning of a tale of innocence

exploited. Little Nell, we learn, is 'nearly fourteen', guile-less with a sweet nature. She is her feeble grandfather's companion, the one doting on the other and *vice versa*. Through gambling, however, her grandfather has fallen into debt to a moneylender called Daniel Quilp, about whom everything is dirty, crooked and ugly. Quilp – 'so low in stature as to be quite a dwarf, though his head and face were large enough for the body of a giant' – lusts after Little Nell who, unsurprisingly, is terrified by him.

Forced out of their old curiosity shop Little Nell and her grandfather are reduced to begging and wandering the byways of England. Even there, though, they are not safe. Wrongly convinced that the old man has hoarded a fortune for Nell, her brother Frederick enlists Dick Swiveller to help him track down the couple so that Swiveller can marry her and the two can share Nell's non-existent inheritance. Quilp agrees to help, not because he thinks there is a fortune to be made, but in order to revel in the misery he foresees overtaking all concerned.

As the story unfolded readers could barely contain their impatience to know what happened next. Not for the first time, and certainly not for the last, Dickens had found a character with whom readers could sympathet-ically identify. Little Nell was one child among many whom Victorian society had failed.

Deaths of children were so commonplace as to be hardly noticed. In 1839, a year before Dickens started to write *The Old Curiosity Shop*, half of the funerals in London were for children younger than ten years of age. Danger was there aplenty for those unable or without the means to look after themselves.

At one point in the novel Quilp, who epitomises evil, tells his lawyer, the well-named Mr Brass, to watch how he goes as he leaves his yard. 'Be sure to pick your way among the timber, for all the rusty nails are upwards. There's a dog in the lane. He bit a man last night, and a woman the night before, and last Tuesday he killed a child – but that was in play. Don't go too near him.'

Little Nell herself, Dickens suggested, was modelled on his beloved sister-in-law Mary Hogarth, who died at the age of seventeen and who was much in his thoughts as he wrote the novel. Indeed, so upset was he at Nell's approaching death that he spun out the narrative to delay the inevitable. No one, he said, would miss her more than he would, indicating just how close the relationship can be between a writer and one of his characters.

'It is such a painful thing to me, that I can only express my sorrow,' he said. 'Old wounds bleed afresh when I only think of the way of doing it: what the actual doing it will be, God knows. . . Dear Mary died yesterday when I think of this sad story.'

But Dickens, despite his reservations, knew what he must do. It was in his power to save Nell but he knew he must not and could not. Little Nell's premature death was assured from the moment she first appeared on the page. To let her live would be to deny reality and give way to sentimentality. For the sake of the novel's integrity it was essential she must die.

The impact, though, was stupendous. Lord Jeffrey was not alone in breaking down in tears. William Macready, the actor, was grief-stricken, not least because his own daughter had died recently. Daniel O'Connell, the Irish statesman, threw his copy of *Master Humphrey's Clock* out of a train window, shouting, 'He should not have killed her!' In New York, meanwhile, crowds gathered at the harbour to ask passengers from England for news of Nell's fate. When told it many wept. For every critic who felt that Dickens had gone emotionally overboard there were tens of thousands of others who were distraught. To them, Nell's plight was all too familiar and all too immediate.

The chord that Dickens had struck confirmed him as England's greatest living novelist. In the opinion of many he was to the novel what Shakespeare was to plays. Portraits made of him around this period show him to be still youthful. Clean-shaven and clear-eyed, his locks flowing girlishly, he looks at the age of thirty to have the world at his feet, which he surely had. He now decided it was time he saw the United States, taking with him his wife and four children, all of whom were under five years of age. His wife was not keen; Dickens was adamant. And so they went, travelling by steam packet from Liverpool to Boston. It was not a trip for the faint-hearted. Dickens suffered dreadfully from seasickness but Dickens being Dickens did not have it in 'the ordinary acceptation of the term'. At Boston the boat was boarded by reporters, which set the tone for the entire visit.

Treated like royalty wherever he went, Dickens lapped it all up. 'I can give you no conception of my welcome here,' he told an English friend. 'There never was a king or an emperor upon the earth so cheered and followed by crowds, and entertained in public at splendid balls and dinners.'

It would be wrong, however, to think that all Americans swooned in his presence. Some thought him coarse, and a cracker of bad jokes, others regarded him as aloof, arrogant and a bit of a dandy. He was, moreover, critic-ised in the newspapers for complaining about the American disregard of copyright to the financial detri-ment of writers such as himself. Inevitably, Dickens got a book out of his trip, *American Notes*, which was not one of his best, perhaps because he was always on display. Similarly, when he visited Italy a few years later the resulting book was rather dull. He was not, it seems, a born travel writer.

Little Nell's Death

Yet he could not turn off his writing tap. Words poured out of him in a gush for, apart from anything else, he did not want his public to forget him. Out of the American visit, too, came a novel, *Martin Chuzzlewit*, which may not be his finest (though he thought it was at the time), but does contain some of the most sublimely comic episodes in all of his work and two of the most memorable characters, Pecksniff and Mrs Gamp.

Like its predecessors, it first appeared serially but sales were slow, probably because the opening chapter – 'concerning the Pedigree of the Chuzzlewit Family' – was verbose and unfunny. As sales began to flag Dickens sought to revive them. But what to do? Writers of detective novels, when faced with a flagging plot, are told to follow Raymond Chandler's example and send a man into a room carrying a gun. That, it was believed, was guaranteed to seize the reader's attention. This was never an option for Dickens.

Ought he, he pondered, thinking how he might spice up his plot, to attack the owners of tin mines in Cornwall or concentrate his ire on abuses in child employment? In the end neither appealed. Instead Dickens decided to send Martin Chuzzlewit to America, which proved inspired, because it was somewhere his English readers had never been while it would help cement his relationship with their American counterparts.

In the beginning, however, was the hero's name. As Peter Ackroyd and others have observed, names were very important to Dickens. For him, they helped define character. 'On a sheet of paper,' wrote Ackroyd, 'he transcribed all the titles of his previous novels, and then he wrote Martin chuzzlewig, then Martin chubblewig, then chuzzletoe and chuzzlebog. Then on another sheet he wrote down a whole range of surnames; Martin was clearly right, but now he put after it chuzzlewig, Sweezleden, chuzzletoe, Sweezlebach, Sweeezlewag. Then he decides on Chuzzlewig, writing out a longer title, only to change his mind and on another sheet put Martin Chuzzlewit. He had found it.'

It was a small battle won in a war which Dickens was waging on many fronts. Publishers were wooing him. He helped form the Society of Authors, which to this day continues to fight for writers' rights. His father was again up to his old tricks, spending more money than he owned. Moved by the death of an actor he knew Dickens arranged a benefit performance of *Hamlet* for his children. There was always something to worry about or rouse him or niggle away at his conscience.

Wandering through the slums of London he came across what were known as Ragged Schools, where poor children were being taught by well-meaning masters. Instantly Dickens decided he must help raise funds for this laudable institution and began to call in favours from well-to-do friends. But even as he was throwing himself into this project another idea for a book began to germinate. At first, he thought of writing a pamphlet and got as far as giving it a title: *An Appeal to the People of England on behalf of the Poor Man's Child*. 'Happily,' as the novelist John Mortimer observed, 'he changed his mind and decided to channel his anger into a Christmas story which would last forever.'

This was none other than *A Christmas Carol*, which has become a key part of what's regarded as a traditional Christmas. How to describe what Christmas was like in 1843? Perhaps the best way is simply to say it was nothing like it is now. For instance, Christmas trees were only to be found in the homes of the upper classes where their popularity grew because Queen Victoria liked to have one.

No one sent Christmas cards, because they hadn't been invented. The first such cards arrived in 1843 and featured an illustration of a family with a small child drinking wine together. Moreover there was only one day's holiday, and not even that in Scotland, and present-giving was yet to become the joy and the chore it is for us now.

For Dickens it was not so much a religious festival as an opportunity to spoil children, to shower on them all the attention and affection so many of them did not receive throughout the rest of the year. While he had no trouble in imagining what it was like to be a child, taking every chance he had to behave like one, he felt that other adults had long forgotten.

Their representative is Ebenezer Scrooge, whose surname has become synonymous with miserliness. But not only is he mean, he also a killjoy. To him the very idea of people enjoying and indulging themselves is abhorrent.

'Out upon merry Christmas!' he rages. 'What's Christmas Time to you but a time for paying bills without money; a time for finding yourself a year older and not an hour richer; a time for balancing your books and having every item in 'em through a round dozen of months presented dead against you. If I could work my will. . . every idiot who goes about with "Merry Christmas" on his lip, should be boiled with his own pudding, and buried with a stake of holly through his heart. He should!'

Nothing, as John Mortimer has said, had ever before been published like *A Christmas Carol*. For reasons that are probably beyond explanation the public adopted it as they might a baby abandoned on a doorstep. Dickens, it seemed, was speaking directly to them, telling a story as he might to his own family around the fireplace. It was direct, funny, scary, brilliant, the tone set from the opening sentence: 'Marley was dead: to begin with.'

Dickens, noted Mortimer, did not always receive good

reviews for his books but there were no bad ones for *A Christmas Carol*. 'Thackeray, writing in *Fraser's Magazine*, called it a "national benefit". The *Sunday Times* called it "sublime", and an American factory owner gave his workers an extra day's holiday when he had finished reading it.'

Six thousand copies of the first edition were sold the day the book was published. Dickens had every right to feel jubilant. He could clear his debts and look forward, or so he supposed, to a windfall when the profits started to come in. But as authors before and since have learned to appreciate hoped-for cash does not always translate into the real thing.

Expecting to make at least £1000, Dickens earned just £230 for the first edition. The night he got the bad news, he said, he 'slept as badly as Macbeth'. He was incandescent with anger at his publishers and fuming at plagiarists who undermined sales of the original of *A Christmas Carol* with cheap and nasty copies. At the time it must have hurt him deeply. The only compensation was that he had written a classic.

CHAPTER SEVEN

The First 'Major' Novel

IN the mid-nineteenth century travel became widely available for the first time. Before then, only the rich, the adventurous or the foolhardy were interested in visiting the town nearest to where they lived let alone in going abroad. Indeed, many people spent their entire lives living in the place in which they were born and never for a moment felt they had been deprived or had missed out. That, though, all changed in a few frantic decades.

First came the mass exodus of people from the countryside to the towns. Then there was the invention of steam power and, as a consequence, the arrival of the railway, which drastically reduced journey times and made travelling considerably cheaper. In the early 1830s the first train to carry passengers was introduced, from

Liverpool to Manchester. Ten years later what was initially regarded as being as dangerous as mounting a bucking bronco had become an increasingly accepted and popular way to get around.

Foreign travel, however, was still relatively rare but that, too, was soon to change, thanks to Thomas Cook, a religious teetotaller, whose 'tours' were expressly designed to shield tourists from the bugbears, real and imaginary, of countries such as Greece and Italy, France and Spain.

It was Italy that Dickens longed to see and if he must see it so too must his family, whether they wanted to or not. He asked a friend who was living there to help with accommodation, ideally a palazzo in Pisa, famed for its Leaning Tower. 'Here,' Dickens wrote, 'is a list of the caravan:

- The inimitable Boz.
- The other half ditto.
- The sister of ditto ditto.
- Four babies, ranging from two years and a half to seven and a half.
- Three women servants, commanded by Anne of Broadstairs.'

There was another baby, Francis Jeffrey, but he was reckoned to be too young to undertake such a journey. Later, however, he was added to the caravan, which set off, after a grand farewell dinner, on 2nd July, 1844.

Dickens could scarcely contain his excitement, weary as he was of England, his commitments and the constraints and conceits of the class system. In Italy, he imagined himself reinvented and reinvigorated, dressed 'in a striped shirt, moustache, blouse, red sash, straw hat, and white trousers, sitting astride a mule, and not caring for the clock, the day of the month or the day of the week.'

As it turned out Dickens rented a house in Genoa, in the north-west corner of Italy, from where he toured the rest of the boot-shaped country. He was no connoisseur of art or antiquity; his interest was in observing the people for whom the famous sights were merely a backdrop. For passport purposes he described himself as having a 'fair' complexion, 'very cheerful' eyes, with a 'not supercilious' nose, 'smiling' mouth, 'beaming' visage and an 'extremely agreeable' general expression. Which sounds like the attitude of a man intent on enjoying a holiday. Nor, it seems, was he disappointed.

The telescope-shaped Leaning Tower did not warrant more than passing comment from him. He preferred to dwell on the city's numerous beggars. At Carrara, from whose surrounding hills Michelangelo quarried the marble for his statue of David, he was impressed by the performance at the opera, which was 'unlike the common people of Italy generally, who (with some exceptions among the Neapolitans) sing vilely out of tune, and have very disagreeable singing voices'. He was moved by Pompeii's 'deadly lonesomeness', visited – how typical of Dickens – a prison in Florence and reported on the stabbing to death of a seventeen-year-old girl by an old man of eighty. In Rome he attended a mass conducted by the Pope, which seemed to last for ever: 'Not because it takes long to bless a candle through and through, but because there were so many candles to be blessed.'

Dickens, it is safe to presume, was not a religious man. In his introduction to *Pictures From Italy*, the inevitable product of his year-long stay, he pre-empted criticism from those of the Roman Catholic faith, saying: 'When I hint a dislike of nunneries for young girls who abjure the world before they have ever proved or known it; or doubt the *ex officio* sanctity of all Priests and Friars; I do no more than many conscientious Catholics both abroad and at home.'

IT WAS not long after his return to England that Dickens embarked on his next novel. *Dombey and Son* has been described by the influential critics F.R. and Q.D. Leavis as his first 'major' novel. What they meant by this controversial statement they must themselves be allowed to explain.

'*Dombey and Son*,' they wrote in 1970, 'marks a decisive moment in Dickens's career; he offered it as a providently conceived whole, presenting a major theme, and it was his first essay in the elaborately plotted Victorian novel.' What I think the Leavises were trying to say was that here is a novel which, unlike Dickens's previous books, was thought through from start to finish. He did not improvise as he went along. He knew at the outset where he was going and what he wanted to say and how.

To help him concentrate and to give him perspective he again left England, travelling first to Switzerland, then to France. In the Alps he began to map out his detailed plans for *Dombey and Son*.

'He was planning so far in advance, in fact, that he knew what part of the story he would have reached by the time he arrived in Paris some five or six months later,' wrote Peter Ackroyd. 'Certainly the novel itself bears all the signs of prior construction, and on the very first page he characterises Dombey himself as "a tree that was to come down in good time", from the beginning, too, his prose here is marked by a deliberation and restraint that were not so readily apparent in his earlier fictions.'

The major 'theme' to which the Leavises alluded was pride which, as everyone knows, comes before a fall. At the core of the novel is Mr Paul Dombey, whose company gives it its title. A driven businessman, to him everything is a transaction. With no mother to feed his frail infant son, also named Paul, he employs a wet nurse, to whom he makes clear the nature of their arrangement. 'When you go away from here you will have concluded what is a mere matter of bargain and sale, of hiring and letting, and will stay away.'

Everything and everyone, he believes, has a price. In that regard, Mr Dombey symbolised for Dickens the *laissez-faire* approach to business, and life in general, to which many Victorians subscribed. But he is not a contented man, doomed as he is to reflect on the loss of his son, wise beyond his years and dead at the age of six. Travelling alone by train Mr Dombey has time to think and brood. 'He found no pleasure or relief in the journey,' writes Dickens.

> 'Tortured by these thoughts he carried monotony with him, through the rushing landscape, and hurried headlong, not through a rich and varied country, but a wilderness of blighted plans and gnawing jealousies. The very speed at which the train was whirled along mocked the swift course of the young life that had been borne away so steadily and so inexorably to its foredoomed end. The power that forced itself upon its iron way – its own – defiant of all paths and roads, pierced through the heart of every obstacle, and dragging living creatures of all classes, ages and degrees behind it, was a type of the triumphant monster, Death.'

This short extract gives some hint of the darkness that lies at the core of *Dombey and Son*. The train is carrying Mr Dombey to oblivion. Moreover, it is the apt symbol of an age in a hurry. Trains do not go round obstacles. Rather they bulldoze their way through them, the object being to get as quickly as possible from A to B. They run on a set path to a predetermined timetable. Where possible, chance is eliminated. Yet, ironically, for the period in which you are a passenger there is, however briefly, the opportunity to take stock, to consider where your life is going and where it has been, as the scenery flashes past in a blur.

In writing about Mr Dombey, it is hard not to believe that Dickens was thinking about himself, about his career, his past, and his life with his wife and children. Clearly, he was in reflective mood, nearing middle age, that breakwater between youth and decline.

Dickens finished the novel, which ran to nearly nine hundred pages, in the spring of 1848, and declared himself satisfied with it. It would, he rightly thought, 'be remembered and read years hence'. Any doubts he had that his powers were waning were dispelled.

Like its seven predecessors, *Dombey and Son* was lapped up by his loyal readers. Dickens now was a writer in his prime, confident in his own powers and in his ability to take readers with him wherever he chose to go. It is a mark of all great artists, to be always willing to take risks, confound expectations and spring surprises. Often the best praise they receive is that their latest work is nothing like that which came before it.

OVER THE COURSE of the next few years, as the nineteenth century approached and passed its mid-point, Dickens developed from an immensely gifted writer into a truly great one. There are many critics who believe that he reached his peak in 1850 with the publication of *David Copperfield*.

The Russian novelist, Leo Tolstoy, was one of them, often referring to it and acknowledging it as a mighty influence on his own writing. Dickens himself felt the story 'to its minutest point', which suggests that of all his novels this was the one that followed most closely his own life journey. In fact, some critics have suggested that there is no need to read biographies of Dickens because he wrote his own and called it *David Copperfield*. That, though, is to encourage us to read it for what it tells us about its author when we ought to read to discover what it says about ourselves.

It begins, as several of Dickens's novels do, with a boy being born. The story is told in the first person which immediately allows readers to identify with whoever that is, which, in this case, is David Copperfield. The early chapters all have the word 'I' in their title: I am Born; I Observe; I have a Chance; I fall into Disgrace; I am sent away from Home, etc. David is telling his story and telling it in a leisurely fashion, as if he wants to savour it as richly as he wants us to. No detail is spared, no aside ignored, no random thought dismissed.

David, again like so many of Dickens's fictional children, is a parent short or, as he puts it: 'I was a post-humous child.' More often than not a mother is missing, having died in childbirth. In David Copperfield's case, however, it is his father who is no more. 'My father's eyes,' he relates, 'had closed upon the light of this world six months when mine opened on it. There is something strange to me, even now, in the reflection that he never saw me; and something stranger yet in the shadowy remembrance that I have of my first childish associations with his white gravestone in the churchyard'.

As we turn the pages we see how David's mother is wooed by Mr Murdstone, who quickly moves his own mother into the household, to David's distress. Soon David is sent away to school, returning home only for holidays. Again the chapter titles lead with the word 'I': I have a Memorable Birthday; I become Neglected, and am provided for; I begin Life on my own Account, and don't like it. The question posed by David at the beginning of the novel is whether he will be 'the hero' of his own life, or whether 'that station will be held by anyone else'.

While offering that tantalising prospect Dickens was in no doubt where *David Copperfield* lay in the hierarchy of his affections. 'Like many fond parents,' he said, 'I have a favourite child and his name is David Copperfield.'

BUT EVEN as he was putting the final touches to the novel Dickens was already planning another ambitious venture. He had, he said, a 'dim design' for yet another magazine, of which the Victorian age had a super abundance. As ever more people learned to read, demand grew to meet supply. Dickens, thinking of a cheap, mass-circulation magazine that covered whatever topics took his fancy, hired staff, rented office space and, after much soul-searching, came up with a title: *Household Words*.

Instantly, it was a hit, selling 100,000 copies. Costing just 2d, it was by any standard a bargain. Though its contributors included the likes of Elizabeth Gaskell, famed as the author of *Cranford* (there was 'no living English writer', Dickens said, whose work he wanted to print), and a host of others whose lustre has faded in time, it was the author of *The Pickwick Papers, Oliver Twist* and *A Christmas Carol* who was undoubtedly the major attraction.

Not only did Dickens write many pieces for the magazine, he was forever coming up with ideas for others to execute. Among the many young writers whose work he promoted were George Meredith, Wilkie Collins, who went on to write *The Moonstone* and *The Woman in White* and George Eliot, the pseudonym of Mary Ann Evans, whose novel *Middlemarch* is often cited as the finest ever produced by an English author.

Moreover the variety of subjects covered in *Household Words* was remarkably diverse, from a description of San Francisco in the late 1840s during the Gold Rush, to the use of ice for preserving food and the possibility of crossing the English Channel by tunnel or a series of bridges. It was, however, its devotion to highlighting social problems that marked out the magazine.

'Hardly a week goes by,' noted another of Dickens's biographers, Edgar Johnson, 'in which it is not attacking some abuse.' The targets – illiteracy, prejudice, the need for a proper sewage system, reform of prisons, decent housing, to name but a few – were many. Chief among them perhaps was the importance of education, a cause very near to Dickens's heart. In article after article he returned to the subject and in so doing managed to change public opinion and improve the lives of countless people for the better.

'Week after week,' wrote Johnson, 'Dickens or his henchmen hammered away, wielding every conceivable weapon: reasoned argument, cajolery, facts and figures, humour, insinuation, irony, parable and allegory, sarcasm, repetition, angry diatribe.' He was the ultimate campaigner and the most eloquent and persuasive of advocates, able to debate at whatever level was appropriate. Not without reason did Lord Northcliffe, who founded the *Daily Mail*, judge Dickens to be the greatest magazine editor not just of his own time but of any time.

CHAPTER EIGHT

Human Spontaneous Combustion

THERE are countless ways in which a writer can dispose of a character who has outlived his or her usefulness. He can push them under trains, throw them off bridges, bury them alive, have them eaten by cannibals or animals or by their best friends. If he feels so inclined he could even frighten, starve or choke them to death. Or all three. In *Bleak House*, however, Dickens did away with a character in a wholly original manner. Eager to be rid of Mr Krook, the alcoholic owner of a rag-and-bone shop, he killed him off by means of human spontaneous combustion.

There is much in Dickens's work that seems unlikely but nothing quite as bizarre as Krook's explosive demise. Unsurprisingly, critics heaped scorn on such a convenient turn of events, arguing that spontaneous combustion of a human being was so implausible as to be plain daft. Dickens, however, was unfazed.

'I have no need to observe that I do not wilfully or negligently mislead my readers,' he protested, 'and that before I wrote that description I took pains to investigate.'

Whether human spontaneous combustion is scientifically possible is actually neither here nor there. What matters is that we are persuaded by what we read. What is required is what the poet Samuel Taylor Coleridge called a 'willing suspension of disbelief'. It is enough proof for a writer that something, however outrageous or fantastic or unusual, can happen once. That is the nature of fiction. As we read a novel we need to be aware that many of the things that happen in its pages are unlikely to happen elsewhere. In other words, they're extraordinary, which is why we find reading about them so fascinating.

No one knew this better than Dickens. If nothing else the incident in *Bleak House* got people talking. And what a great novel it is. Published as usual in monthly parts, between March 1852 and September 1853, it was for many of the author's admirers their favourite of his novels, including as it does the legendary court case of Jarndyce v Jarndyce, in which members of a family are locked in a seemingly endless dispute over their inheritance. Such cases, as Dickens knew well, were all too common, their only beneficiaries being the lawyers in whose interests it was to keep them alive for as long as possible.

This forms the spine of the novel and is the subject of wonderfully ripe satire. But what is equally memorable is Dickens's loving descriptions of nineteenth century London, to which he returned again and again in his novels, using the traditional murkiness of its weather as a metaphor for the capital's choking commercialism, suffocating bureaucracy and teeming streets.

'Fog everywhere,' writes Dickens on the opening page.

> 'Fog up the river, where it flows among green aits and meadows; fog down the river, where it rolls defiled among the tiers of shipping, and the waterside pollution of a great (and dirty) city. Fog on the Essex marshes, fog on the Kentish heights. Fog creeping into the cabooses of collier-brigs; fog lying out on the yards, and hovering in the rigging of great ships; fog drooping on the gunwales of barges and small boats. Fog in the eyes and throats of ancient Greenwich pensioners, wheezing by the firesides of their wards; fog in the stem and bowl of the afternoon pipe of the wrathful skipper, down in his close cabin; fog cruelly pinching the toes and fingers of his shivering little 'prentice boy on deck. Chance people on the bridges peeping over the parapets into a nether sky of fog, with fog all round them, as if they were up in a balloon, and hanging in the misty clouds.'

This is as near to poetry as prose gets. It is easy to imagine Dickens composing such passages, setting the scene for the story to follow, enticing readers into his web, intoxicating them with the sheer exuberance of his language. It is a *tour de force* that immediately pricks our interest and grips us like a vice.

The writing of *Bleak House* coincided with Dickens himself moving house, which was always stressful. His children were growing rapidly; the eldest, Mamey, was fourteen. While he wrote and directed how rooms should be organised – like many writers, he was fanatically tidy – he was simultaneously engaged in several other projects. A theatre company which he had recently founded went from success to success. He was instrumental in the foundation of the Guild of Literature and Art, a precursor of such organisations as the Royal Society of Literature and the Society of Authors. There were slums to be cleared, blocks of flats to be built. Not only was he prepared to criticise the conditions in which many people were forced to live but he was determined to do what he could about it.

Meanwhile, his own health was not good. For example, he suffered terribly from kidney trouble. Every book sapped his energy. After completing *Bleak House*, he said: 'I should be lying in the sunshine by the hour together if there were such a thing.' He was weary and needed rest. So off again he went to Italy, to recharge his batteries and think about what he wanted to do next. An idea, he said, had gripped him 'by the throat in a very violent manner'. What he wanted to do was 'to strike the heaviest blow in my power' for the victims of mill owners who were condemned to working long and dangerous hours in conditions that degraded human beings.

The result was *Hard Times*, which Dickens set in Coketown, which could have been modelled on any town in the heart of England dominated by industry. Here – in what was known as the Black Country – were chimneys belching sulphurous smoke twenty-four hours a day, where it seemed the sun never shone.

'Coketown' (writes Dickens) 'was a town of red brick, or of brick that would have been red if the smoke and the ashes had allowed it. . .

'. . . but as matters stood it was a town of unnatural red and black like the painted face of a savage. It was a town of machinery and tall chimneys, out of which interminable serpents of smoke trailed themselves for ever and ever, and never got uncoiled. It had a black canal in it, and a river that ran purple with ill-smelling dye, and vast piles of buildings full of windows where there was a rattling and a trembling all day long, and where the piston of the steam-engine worked monotonously up and down like the head of an elephant in a state of melancholy madness. It contained several large streets all very like one another, and many small streets still more like one another, inhabited by people equally like one another, who all went in and out at the same hours, with the same sound upon the pavements, to do the same work, and to whom every day was the same as yesterday and tomorrow, and every year the counterpart of the last and the next.'

Critics tend to dismiss *Hard Times* as a minor Dickens novel and have suggested that it is his 'least read' and most unconvincing. This may be true; alternatively it may be nonsense. All we can do is read it for ourselves. In the interests of research Dickens travelled north, going by way of Wolverhampton and Birmingham to Preston, through a 'blackened' landscape that had been forged in the past few decades. At Preston, there was a long-running strike among workers in the cotton mills. Dickens thought it an awful place and was bored and depressed.

The novel he wrote was much shorter than usual. Everyone who has read it remembers Mr Gradgrind, the schoolmaster who droned facts into his pupils until they couldn't see a horse for its hooves. It is a masterly satire of a certain kind of teacher of whom there were countless numbers. For Dickens he was an unmissable target.

What saved the novel, according to Dingle Foot, who in 1955 provided an introduction to it, was two characters, Mrs Sparsit and Bounderby.

'To anyone born in the first decade of the twentieth century (wrote Foot), 'they are still recognisable figures.

'. . . No doubt by the end of the century they will have ceased to be so. Possibly the aristocratic snobbery of Mrs. Sparsit will still remain in some few remote backwaters of our island. But the inverted snob, who glories in the lowliness of his early years, must most certainly disappear. Already he is a type which is passing away. The Log Cabin to the White House epic has become too familiar to produce anything but a yawn. But a century ago the self-made man who brazenly claimed to owe everything to his own exertions must have been an extremely familiar figure.'

Dickens himself, it should be pointed out, was some-thing of a snob. His, however, was an odd and now faded – if not quite disappeared – kind of snobbery, that of what Foot called 'the English commercial middle class'.

Dickens's snobbery was most definitely not of the kind that wanted to find favour from the aristocracy. Like P.G. Wodehouse, creator of Jeeves and Bertie Wooster, Dickens always enjoyed making fun of the upper classes. His lords and ladies are often objects of derision whose behaviour he found unintentionally comic. He had contempt for titles and regarded uniforms as others might a clown's costume. But his greatest derision was reserved for those who adopted the attitudes, postures and accents of those who belonged to what was seen as a superior class. At heart he was a meritocrat, who had won his place in the world by his own endeavours rather than through who his father was or by inheritance.

In Coketown and its ilk there was scant chance to rise. It was the sort of place that deadened the spirits and denied ambition. Survival was the best many of its inhabitants could hope for. It was hard enough to get from one end of a day to the other. The only respite on offer was the occasional trip to the countryside where it was green and trees grew and larks sang. Even then, though, Coketown loomed large, casting ashes 'not only on its own head but on the neighbourhood's too'.

For someone as sensitive as Dickens it was a bleak prospect. It was, he thought, evil. The greed. The disregard for fellow human beings. The ruination of England's green and pleasant land. The turning of men and women into machines. The lack of charity, the pursuit of money.

For Dickens, who was a natural optimist, such thoughts were lowering. Nor was it easy to find reasons for hope. The Crimean War started in 1854, pushing reform at home off the agenda. His magazine, *Household Words*, was going through a sticky patch. The same might be said of his marriage to Catherine who was prone to depression. On top of all of which one of their daughters,

Mary, was taken desperately ill with cholera, reminding them of the earlier loss of another daughter, Dora, in infancy.

During the summer of 1854, 20,000 people in England and Wales had died from the highly contagious disease, which could be traced directly to poor sanitation, polluted water and crowded living conditions. But how could those people most affected – the poor and the working class – bring about change when most of them had no vote? Dickens was frustrated, enraged, impatient for progress.

Yet he went on writing. And what did he write about? About society and its relationship to individuals and how their will is bent to suit its needs. His next novel, *Little Dorrit*, began to appear in December 1855 and ran monthly until June 1857. Much of it is situated in prisons, whether it's the Marshalsea, the debtors' prison where his father was kept, or one in Marseilles, or prisons of the mind, such as the monastery of St Bernard or the Circumlocution Office, the most important of governmental departments, whose finger, writes Dickens, 'was in the largest public pie, and the smallest public tart'.

'This glorious establishment,' he adds, 'had been early in the field, when the one sublime principle involving the difficult art of governing a country, was first distinctly revealed to statesmen. It had been foremost to study that bright revelation, and to carry its shining influence through the whole of official proceedings. Whatever was required to be done, the Circumlocution Office was beforehand with all the public departments in the art of perceiving – HOW NOT TO DO IT.'

To read such passages, more than 150 years after they were first written, is to realise that there is very little that is new under the sun. Certainly, anyone who has seen the TV series *Yes Minister* will recognise what Dickens is talking about. Of course, he exaggerated, but the more scorn he poured the more real and truthful became the targets of it. It has been said by several scholars of Dickens that he himself felt imprisoned at this time, strapped in a straitjacket of his own making.

Like him, his heroine, whose real name is Amy, has a father who is in the Marshalsea. Unlike him, however, she grew up there. There appears be no way out of his predicament for William Dorrit but the discovery that he is the lost heir to a fortune – a typical Dickensian solution – secures his release. Thereafter the Dorrits go on tour around Europe, as, conveniently, had the Dickenses. But the sudden wealth does not make him or the other Dorrits, with the exception of Amy, better people.

Eventually Amy, again like too many of Dickens's

heroes and heroines, is left all alone. In a plot that has more twists in it than a pretzel, and with the discovery of another lost fortune, Amy becomes the recipient of another huge legacy which, it turns out, she declines.

The moral of the story may seem too obvious – money does not necessarily bring contentment – but that does not do justice to the complexity of a novel that was born of rage and written with a struggle. For Dickens had so much he wanted to say in it, so many scores he wanted to settle, so many injustices and issues he wanted to confront. One such was the hubris and corruption of bankers, such as Mr Merdle, who in so many respects reminds one of the infamous Wall Street conman, Bernie Madoff:

> 'For, by that time it was known that the late Mr Merdle's complaint had been, simply, Forgery and Robbery. He, the uncouth object of such wide-spread adulation, the sitter at great men's feasts, the roc's egg of great ladies' assemblies, the subduer of exclusiveness, the leveller of pride, the patron of patrons, the bargain-driver with a Minister for Lordships of the Circumlocution Office, the recipient of more acknowledgement within some ten or fifteen years, at most, than had been bestowed in England upon all peaceful public benefactors, and upon all the leaders of all the Arts and Sciences, with all their works to testify for them, during two centuries at least – he, the shining

wonder, the new constellation to be followed by wise men bringing gifts, until it stopped over certain carrion at the bottom of a bath and disappeared – was simply the greatest Forger and the greatest Thief that ever cheated the gallows.'

CHAPTER NINE
Unfinished Business

IN 1859 Dickens closed *Household Words* and replaced it with *All the Year Round*. Taking its lead from Shakespeare – 'The story of our lives, from year to year' – the new magazine started the way its editor meant it to go on, with a bang. The first few pages of each issue were to be given over to a serial and Dickens began by including the first chapter of his latest novel, *A Tale of Two Cities* whose opening lines – 'It was the best of times, it was the worst of times, it was the age of wisdom, it was the age of foolishness,' etc – have become as familiar as a jingle.

By this point in his life Dickens was at the height of his powers as a writer but his personal life was ragged. His marriage to Catherine, which had been deteriorating for some time, was now regarded by him as a prison from which it seemed to him impossible to escape, bound as he was by the conventions of the time. Hence, it has been claimed, his identifying in *A Tale of Two Cities* with a prisoner who has been in jail for years. In fact, Catherine and he had separated the year before the novel saw the light of day.

In part, *A Tale of Two Cities* is about love and the self-sacrifices that it sometimes necessitates. This is personified by Sydney Carton and his doomed pursuit of Lucie Manette. That Dickens, who was then infatuated with the young actress Ellen Ternan, identified with Sydney, a gifted barrister but lacking in self-discipline and willpower, is too tempting an assumption to resist. In the preface to the novel he confessed: 'Through its execution, it has had complete possession of me; I have so far verified what is done and suffered in these pages, as that I have certainly done and suffered it myself.'

Yet again Dickens was guilty of exaggeration. Only superficially can his experience be likened to Sydney's who, after all, goes to the guillotine for his love of Lucie. What Dickens was doing though, as he wrote the novel, was acting out every scene, putting himself into the action, suffering when Sydney suffered. There was surely something of the martyr about him.

Set during the French Revolution, *A Tale of Two Cities* is a historical novel, which was a rare departure for its

author who preferred to write about times he knew. For
that reason it may not be one of his best. Be that as it
may, it is still essential reading. As Peter Ackroyd has
said, 'For those who wish to understand something of
the true nature of Charles Dickens, as one important
aspect of his genius, *A Tale of Two Cities* is a necessary
book.'

Dickens was now nearing fifty, which is not old by
modern standards. In the nineteenth century, however,
it was a significant watershed, given that it was more
usual to die before one reached that age than after it.
Time that has passed cannot be regained except by
memory. Dickens needed no one to tell him that he had
already lived more years than he could expect to see;
his past was longer than his future. How much such
thoughts influenced him is impossible to say. What we
do know is that he was a man in a hurry who, when he
got inspiration for a novel could no more not start writing
it than he could live without breathing.

The novel he had in mind was *Great Expectations*,
which he described to fellow novelist, Henry James, as
'a very fine, new, and grotesque idea'. That recent sales
of *All the Year Round* had been falling merely added to
the necessity to get on with it. Once again he would ride
to a magazine's rescue. In a letter to John Forster, his
son-in-law, in which he enclosed the first instalment, he
explained:

'The book will be written in the first person throughout, and during these first three weekly numbers you will find the hero to be a boy-child, like David [Copperfield]. Then he will be an apprentice. You will not have to complain of the want of humour as in the *A Tale of Two Cities*. I have made the opening, I hope, in general effect exceedingly droll. I have put a child and a good-natured foolish man, in relations that seem to me very funny.'

Great Expectations is yet again the story of a boy without parents. His name is Philip Pirrip but he is known by his nickname, Pip. His only living blood relative is his sister, Mrs Joe Gargery, a hard taskmistress. The Gargerys live within a stone's throw of the Kentish marshes, which have been compared to the Yorkshire moors in Emily Bronte's novel, *Wuthering Heights*. There are other similarities between these two evergreen English novels. Bronte's masterpiece had appeared thirteen years before Dickens's and it made a huge impression on him. That, at least, is what we are inclined to believe. But Dickens said he'd never read it or *Jane Eyre* by Emily's sister, Charlotte, which seems unlikely, given how popular and critically acclaimed they were.

Pip's progress is that of a boy ungrateful for the kindness of others. His expectations for himself are indeed great but they are often wrong-headed and prompted by delusions of wealth and status. First person narrators are famously unreliable, in that they offer a portrait of themselves which would not stand cross examination in a court. Pip's testimony is that of someone who cannot see that he is damning himself when he thinks he is damning others. His improvement as a person, his progress, comes through experience and age and he is rewarded by being reunited with his childhood sweetheart Estella after she has separated from her husband.

It was an ending that caused Dickens much sleepless-ness and which many readers thought was too sugary and sentimental. Originally, his intention was for Pip to lose Estella, to realise, as Edgar Johnson wrote, 'that his love for her had always been mad and hopeless, and know that they could never have been happy together.' He was persuaded otherwise by his friend and fellow novelist Edward Bulwer Lytton who felt that Dickens owed it to his readers to give them a happy ending. On balance, he was right.

THERE WAS probably no more famous man in England than Dickens. He was rich – he could command £1000 for a short story, which even in the Victorian era was a huge sum – and he was living at Gad's Hill in Kent, the house he had longed to occupy since he'd been a boy. He had proved that he could not only inform, entertain and amuse, but could influence governments and improve living conditions for countless people. He was loved and respected and, as a writer, could claim to have both popular and critical success, which is a gift few receive. By and large, he could do as he pleased. He owned and edited a magazine. Publishers waved their cheque books at him as football clubs do today at star players.

What marks him, however, as a great artist was his ability to pursue his own instincts. Like all men he had failings; he could be petulant and arrogant and childish. What he was never, though, was predictable. Thus, at a time when others might be thinking of slowing down, of enjoying the fruits of his labour, Dickens took to the stage, touring the country giving readings. Why? Well, we know that from a young age he had been mad about the theatre. His one regret was that he would have preferred to be an actor rather than an author. He was also, as he grew older, eager to see his audience in front of him. It was not enough for him to know that he was read by millions; he wanted to see them with his own eyes. In the nineteenth century there was just one way to achieve this, by going on the road.

At his best, when not weary or agitated, Dickens was a mesmerising performer. Everywhere he went his show, which comprised selected readings from his novels, was a sellout. Indeed, such was the demand for tickets that unscrupulous promoters occasionally sold more of them than there were seats. This was the case in Edinburgh where Dickens was confronted by chaotic scenes. Eventually those without seats were invited to join him on the platform. All seemed well. Dickens apologised for the delay and inconvenience. Then those in seats complained that they couldn't see him. Having at last satisfied everyone, Dickens read from *Nicholas Nickleby*. 'From the beginning to the end,' he reported, 'they didn't lose one point, and they ended with a great burst of cheering.'

With the notable exception of Mark Twain, no other writer had such pulling power or such presence. But as he entered his last decade, Dickens was obviously not as dynamic as he had been formerly. After *Great Expectations* he completed one more novel, *Our Mutual Friend*, which he began in the winter of 1863. The effort it took to write it nearly undid Dickens, who by the time he had finished it was close to a nervous breakdown. He also almost lost the manuscript in a railway accident. Throughout its writing Dickens was often ill but it is nevertheless a novel full of wit and descriptive verve of which only the 'Inimitable', as he liked to call himself, was capable.

Novels stick in the memory for many reasons. With *Our Mutual Friend* two stand out. First, there is the Thames, England's longest river, on which and down which many people drew their livelihoods, none more so than Lizzie Hexham and her father Jesse, who, like birds of prey, comb it by night in search of bodies.

> 'It's my belief you hate the sight of the very river,' says Jesse.
> 'I – I do not like it, father,' replies Lizzie.
> 'As if it wasn't your living!' adds Jesse. 'As if it wasn't meat and drink to you!'

Then there are the Veneerings, one of Dickens's most comical couples. Who, asked Peter Ackroyd, were the Veneerings? . . .

> 'In a sense the Veneerings were everywhere – in this novel Dickens really confronts for the first time the kind of society which was being established in the latter half of the nineteenth century, a society of plutocrats and financiers, of stock-jobbing and brokering, a society of false values and false lives.'

As their name suggests, the Veneerings are all show and no substance. But why try to paraphrase Dickens? Here is how he introduces them to us:

> 'Mr and Mrs Veneering were bran-new people in a bran-new house in a bran-new quarter of London. Everything about the Veneerings was spick and span new. All their furniture was new, all their friends were new, all their servants were new, their plate was new, their carriage was new, their harness was new, their pictures were new, they themselves were new, they were as newly

married as was lawfully compatible with their having a bran-new baby, and if they had set up a great-grandfather, he would have come home in matting from the Pantechnicon, without a scratch upon him, French-polished to the crown of his head.'

There are many such *tours de force* in *Our Mutual Friend*, which stands in the first rank of Dickens's novels. Certainly, its composition exhausted him and doubtless made him wary of embarking on another project of similar intensity. Writing may be a solitary and sedentary way to make a living but it takes its toll both physically and mentally. Moreover, as Samuel Johnson said, 'what is written without effort is in general read without pleasure.'

When young, writers are often aware of the cost to their health of what they're doing. But as the years go by the wiser ones try to conserve their energy, knowing as they do the effort they must make for every book they write.

Dickens, however, was never good at saying 'no'. The word appears not to have been in his vocabulary. If he could do something, he would. His days did not have twenty four hours but however many he needed to achieve his commitments. For him time was elastic; was he not special, superhuman? And so, after he completed *Our*

Mutual Friend, he threw himself into even more public performances, with catastrophic consequences, dying prematurely, said the French novelist, Andre Maurois, 'from excessive work and excessive activity'.

Dickens being Dickens, however, he could not leave the stage he had built, designed and performed on, without one final curtain call. This was *The Mystery of Edwin Drood*, which he began to write in 1868. Its birth was slow, hampered by his faltering eyesight. Doctors advised him to stop his readings and he did for a while, which allowed him to continue with *Edwin Drood*. He wanted to write a mystery novel, the solution to which would be revealed in the last chapter. The first publicly-employed detectives were in operation and were already featuring in novels, most notably Wilkie Collins's *The Woman in White* and *The Moonstone*, which had appeared in 1868, and which Dickens borrowed heavily from when planning *Edwin Drood*.

Whatever the mystery of Edwin Drood was, its author did not live to explain it. Was Drood murdered? If so, who was his killer? Dickens saw through three monthly episodes of the unfolding story and left material for three further episodes. A further six were projected but unwritten. As with the incomplete work of any great artist speculation over how the mystery would have been resolved was fevered. Many are the theories and many have been the attempts to complete the novel. None, needless to say, satisfactorily matches what we might expect from a genius such as Charles Dickens of whom, for once, the cliché is appropriate. Never shall we see his like again.

What 'Great' Means

CHARLES Dickens died on 9th June, 1870, having suffered a stroke two days earlier. Until he fell ill he was writing, writing, writing, as he had done all his adult life. He was at his beloved Gad's Hill in Rochester, Kent.

'Changes of glorious light from moving boughs,' he wrote, 'songs of birds, scents from gardens, woods, and fields – or, rather, from the one great garden of the whole cultivated island in its yielding time – penetrate the Cathedral, subdue its earthy odour, and preach of the Resurrection and the Life.'

The news of his passing was received similarly to that of Little Nell's, with an outpouring of grief and a sense of disbelief. Except that hers was imaginary and his was all too real. The sorrow was global. It was as if everyone, everywhere knew him personally, as if they were members of his family.

'I never knew an author's death to cause such general mourning,' the American poet Henry Longfellow told John Forster.

Dickens is buried in Poets' Corner in Westminster Abbey, to which thousands flocked to pay homage. Rivers of tears were shed and flowers laid until there was room for no more. Nearby lay Milton and Shakespeare, Chaucer and Dryden, the composer Handel and the historian Macaulay; exalted company for the greatest novelist of his age and, arguably, of any age.

More than one hundred and forty years later, Dickens's reputation has withstood the pummeling of time. None explained his enduring appeal better than G.K. Chesterton. 'Whatever the word "great" means,' wrote Chesterton, 'Dickens was what it means. Even the fastidious and unhappy who cannot read his books without a continuous critical exasperation, would use the word of him without stopping to think. They feel that Dickens is a great writer even if he is not a good writer. He is treated as a classic; that is, as a king who may now be deserted, but who cannot now be dethroned.'

The history of literature, however, is one of acclamation and neglect, survival and denial. Writers whose claim on posterity seemed assured to their contemporaries often fall by the wayside, their books found gathering dust in library stacks, hoping against hope that they will be rediscovered.

Such a fate was suffered by many of Dickens's friends. Who now, for instance, reads William Harrison Ainsworth, Charles Reade, Edward Bulwer Lytton and George Gissing, each of whom had their popular moment? But Dickens was different; Dickens created a world in his own image, in the process of which he populated it with characters, whether good or bad, who came to define Englishness. As the essayist Walter Bagehot said: 'He describes London like a special correspondent for posterity.'

And yet there were those who found him vulgar, who could not quite understand his appeal, who found the way he wrote offensive to their eyes and ears. The Leavises labelled those with such views as 'the blind-bat school of Dickens critics'. Even so, when in his influential and controversial book, *The Great Tradition*, F.R. Leavis called *Hard Times* a masterpiece it provoked a furious debate. What on earth, the blind-bat scholars wanted to know, was Dickens doing in a 'tradition' that included Jane Austen, George Eliot, Henry James and Joseph Conrad?

At present Dickens's reputation stands as high – if not higher – as any of that quartet. His novels are constantly being adapted for the cinema and television. His books remain in print in many editions and all languages. His life is regularly re-examined and re-imagined. Everyone who knew him left a reminiscence, as did many who did not. All that was necessary was to have heard his voice and to have read his words. His unique ability is to make us feel. To read a novel by Dickens is to become emotionally involved, and in that there is no shame. As you read him you cannot help but laugh or cry. You are overcome with anger or sadness or disappointment. Above all you need to know out of sheer curiosity what happens next.

THIS SHORT book has leaned heavily on a few other books that are much longer. For those who wish to read more about Dickens the choice is staggering.

The first biography of him, by John Forster, remains required reading. Forster's access to Dickens was second to none and, moreover, he was writing about his subject while living through his times.

G.K. Chesterton's biography, recently republished in *The Everyman Chesterton*, is the kind of book Dickens himself might have written about an author he admired.

Edgar Johnson's *Charles Dickens: His Tragedy and Triumph*, which was first published in 1952, was for many years the standard modern biography.

In his *Dickens*, which appeared in 1990, Peter Ackroyd brings to his interpretation the sympathetic insight of a fellow novelist and Londoner.

F.R. and Q.D. Leavis's *Dickens the Novelist*, which considers the development of Dickens and his contribution to the art of the novel, has weathered better than most criticism.

None of the above, though, should be read before, or as a substitute for, the novels themselves. All of the quotes from them in this book are taken from the 21-volume edition of *The Oxford Illustrated Dickens*, which was published by Oxford University Press and which offers a lifetime of delight.

Other titles in the
INSPIRATIONS series

John Lennon

the story of the original Beatle

Chris Dolan

John Lennon's life is one of the best known stories in the whole of popular culture. . . and yet there is always an unknown element to his character and his work.

Arguably no other composer or performer had such a profound impact on people. And few other public figures of the last century, from any walk of life, have had so many seemingly separate existences – pop star, spokesman, tragic victim, madman, jester – and genius.

Chris Dolan captures the essence of John Lennon's creative life and work. From a painful and bewildering Liverpool childhood to world renown, his and his fellow Beatles' sheer musicianship and inventiveness, imagination, skill and ambition are awesome. Lennon's life is an inspiration.

ISBN: 978 1 906134 68 6
classification: biography
cover price: £5.99 paperback
extent: 128 pages, colour cover with flaps
size: 178 x 111mm
www.argyllpublishing.co.uk

J K Rowling

the mystery of fiction

Lindsey Fraser

J K Rowling's story is almost as magical as her books. The day she wrote the name Harry Potter on a page she changed not just her own unhappy life but that of millions of readers. Harry Potter and his friends turned Rowling into one of the richest and most influential women in the world. So who is she, and where did her ideas come from? Lindsey Fraser tells the remarkable tale that began one day on a train, when Rowling had forgotten to pack a pen. . .

ISBN: 978 1 906134 69 3
classification: biography
cover price: £5.99 paperback
extent: 128 pages, colour cover with flaps
size: 178 x 111mm
www.argyllpublishing.co.uk

Nelson Mandela

Robben Island to Rainbow Nation

Marian Pallister

Fairness, equality, leadership and justice had been values instilled in prisoner 46664 from his earliest years among his Xhosa people. Nelson Mandela had been a leading figure in the struggle for change in the apartheid state of South Africa. That is why he was in one of the toughest prisons in the world. Robben Island's maximum security prison, built to house political prisoners, offered no escape route. The treatment was brutal and numbers came before names. Yet, more than four decades after his imprisonment the name Mandela continues to be an inspiration in the on-going struggle to create a better world.

ISBN: 978 1 906134 52 5
classification: biography
cover price: £5.99 paperback
extent: 128 pages, colour cover with flaps
size: 178 x 111mm
www.argyllpublishing.co.uk